HOW THE GREAT MOTHER GODDESS EMERGED

(And Keeps on Emerging to Save Us)

RAGHUPATI BHATT

978-0-6452126-1-7

How the Great Mother Goddess Emerged: The Devi Mahatmya

Raghupati Bhatt

MANTICORE PRESS
WWW.MANTICORE.PRESS

CONTENTS

How the Great Mother Emerged is my eleventh book. I selected the Mother Goddess as the theme. I may not be an expert, but I am a devotee. There are already many books on the Mother. However, I opted to concentrate on *Saptashati.* It is my favorite book. I love its enduring poetic quality. Every time I read it, I discover new meanings and interpretations.

I have included a commentary in the form of notes at the end of every chapter, but my word is not the last. Once you enter the *sanctum sanctorum*, a new world will be unveiled before you. Be very reverent. Every word possesses mystical power. The text will be highly revealing if you are respectful towards the Mother.

The world is facing new challenges. The Earth (who is also our Mother) has been very benevolent to all of us. Even though we are exploiting our natural resources, She will find ways to correct us. Yet, I do not think we should lose hope. The future may not shine as brightly now, but the Mother has infinite power. Let us pray to Her in high spirits.

One who turns everything impious into pious,
Shivā, who fulfills all wishes,
We surrender to you
And prostrate before you Narayani

I dedicate this book to –

My mother, Smt. Sarojani
My wife Viji,
My daughters Medha and Srilatha,
And my granddaughter Nihira

KALI THE MOTHER

Swami Vivekananda

The stars are blotted out,
   The clouds are covering clouds,
It is darkness vibrant, sonant.
   In the roaring, whirling wind
Are the souls of a million lunatics
   Just loose from the prison-house,
Wrenching trees by the roots,
   Sweeping all from the path.
The sea has joined the fray,
   And swirls up mountain-waves,
To reach the pitchy sky.
   The flash of lurid light
Reveals on every side
   A thousand, thousand shades
Of Death begrimed and black —
   Scattering plagues and sorrows,
Dancing mad with joy,
   Come, Mother, come!
For Terror is Thy name,
   Death is in Thy breath,
And every shaking step
   Destroys a world for e'er.
Thou "Time," the All-Destroyer!
   Come, O Mother, come!
Who dares misery love,
   And hug the form of Death,
Dance in Destruction's dance,
   To him the Mother comes.

Kali the Mother was written by Swami Vivekananda when he was graced with divine inspiration. His spiritual master, Shri Ramakrishna, was an ardent devotee of Kali and permanently experienced this state.

Swamiji sometimes experienced this trance-like state.

The poem refers to the three aspects of Kali; creation, preservation, and destruction.

The concept of time is also present in Shiva's dance of destruction.

THE MYSTERY OF THE MOTHER GODDESS

God has been worshiped as a Mother in different parts of the world since ancient times. In Goa, we have a sandstone statue of the Mother Goddess, which is several millennia old. Throughout India, there are fifty-one locations devoted to worshiping the Mother Goddess. These centers are known as *shakti peethas. Shakti* means power, and *peetha* means seat. These are literally Seats of Power. Many people believe that this is the oldest form of religious devotion.

Archaeologists have found idols representing the Mother Goddess all over the world. Many of these images have simplistic features. Some scholars believe that in the ancient proto-history of humanity, men were astounded by women's fecundity. Men did not know that they, too, had a role in the process of procreation. People, therefore, attributed supernatural qualities to fertility and worshiped the Mother Goddess. In the early iconography of the Mother, these aspects are very pronounced. All over the world, different names are given to the Goddess. In Egypt, she is Isis. In Greece, she is equated with Aphrodite or Demeter. Some early societies were also matriarchal, and women were the heads of the family.

We do not know precisely when the social structure became patriarchal. Still, there are ample opportunities to demonstrate that early civilizations allocated a lot of importance to the role of the mother. For example, there were *rishis*[1] who were known because of their mothers. There is Satyakam Jabala, whose mother's name was Jabala. The Adityas or the Suns are so-called because their mother's name was Aditi. The Daityas, or the demons, also took their names from their mother, Diti. All the Pandava brothers were called Kaunteya, after their mother, Kunti. Arjuna was also called Partha because his mother, Kunti, had another name – Prutha. Rama is also called Kausaulyey after his mother Kausalya. His brother, Lakshman, is sometimes called Saumitri or Sumitranandan after his mother, Sumitra. The *Ramayana*'s heroine, Sita, was also a Goddess. None can endure like her, for Sita is also regarded as the daughter of the Earth. In one version of the *Ramayana,* it is she who kills Ravana, the demon-king. Krishna also is given names from his mothers Devaki(who gave birth to him) and Yashoda (who raised him).

In some villages, women still honor Gauri, the divine consort of Shiva. There is an all-female festival which goes on for several days, during which the married women return to their parental home. The festival involves singing, dancing, and the celebration of womanhood.

The Earth is also our Mother. She was worshiped in the past and is still revered today. The Moon is also a female Goddess. The rest of the planets, except Venus, are considered to be male. The Moon also has a strong connection with the reproductive physiology of women.

---

[1] The sages who gave expressions to the *ruchas* of the Vedas.

There are other associations, but I do not want to deal with superstitions.

In India, almost all the societies worshiped the Mother in the beginning. They worshiped the Mother as the Goddess of fertility and as a Goddess of wealth. The Mother is *Shakti* or power in India. In Goa, we have a massive sculpture of the Mother Goddess, which is thousands of years old.

There are three forms of the Mother. One is Mahalakshmi. The second is Mahasaraswati, and the third is Mahakali. There are also other forms, and each God also has a female aspect. This female aspect represents the power of that specific God. For example, Aindri represents the power of Indra. Another example is Maheshwari, who embodies the power of Maheshwara or Shankara.

There are several other additional forms, some of which are foreign, and others are associated with tribal deities. There are also forms of the Mother Goddess based on actual people that have been deified later in history and have a historical background. Meenakshi of Madurai was one such historical figure that was deified later. Then there is Sharadamba temple at Shrungeri, which tells us how Sharada fought a verbal battle with Shri Shankaracharya when her husband was defeated. It is believed that Adi Shankara built the temple in memory of Sharada.

The idols of the Mother Goddess have a diverse range of appearances. Many of them are detailed, while others possess minimal features at all.

The Mother Goddess has many forms, including some of whom may have initially been tribal women. There are stories woven around these figures, which indicate a tribal origin.

One form of the Goddess is known as Mariaai. Whenever epidemics and other disasters strike any village, it is called a 'round of Mariaai'. She is an apotropaic deity and is worshiped to prevent epidemics and catastrophes from occurring.

In my childhood, I once saw people coming to our village, begging in the name of Kadaklakshmi. The male member of one of these families wore female garments and held a lasso in his hand. The female had an open chest in which an idol of the Goddess was kept. She would play the drum while the male flagellated himself with the lasso. This act appeared terrible to us because we could see all the scars on his body. We called him Kadaklakshmi, but he is also known as Potraj. Families who belong to a particular caste perform this act. In modern times, however, there has been an awakening amongst the people, and these shows are no longer performed.

In other places, anthills are worshiped as the Mother. Some areas even use large simple stones that are kept in the *sanctum sanctorum,* where they are decorated. Eyes are often added, or a mask is used in these instances of Goddess worship.

I belong to Kolhapur, which is one of the *shakti peethas.* There is a three temple building dedicated to the Goddess Mahalakshmi, which is one thousand three hundred years old. Here Mahalakshmi is worshiped along with Mahakali and Mahasaraswati. There is a book written in

Sanskrit which is of a similar age. Marathi translations of this book also exist.

Later, I went to Ponda Goa, where many temples were dedicated to the Mother Goddess. Shantadurga, Mahalakshmi, Kamakshi, and Mhalasa are the primary forms of the Goddess there. Almost every village in Goa has a temple dedicated to the Mother Goddess. Different names, such as Navadurga or Vijaydurga, are occasionally used, but they are the same. The sacred anthills known as Santeri are also sometimes worshiped in the villages.

Most of these temples are managed by the Saraswat community. Recently there was a controversy about the Navadurga temple in Madkai. The temple management wanted to install a new idol in place of the old one, which is centuries old. The villagers were opposed to this decision.

Then there was a mass movement by the people against the trustees of the temple. Currently, there is a case going on in Ponda court. The hearings continued for days together, and judgment is still awaited. Circumstances such as these indicate that people are very sensitive about the Mother Goddess. There have also been banners declaring, "*Aamchi murti amka jay*" which means, "We want our idol."

I have been a devotee of the Mother Goddess for more than forty years. There is a Sanskrit book known as the *Durga Saptashati* (also known as the *Devi Mahatmya*), which is believed to be a part of a Purana. This may be true. There are seven hundred *shlokas* in the book, which roughly contains *three sections and thirteen chapters.* It reads like a novel, and every chapter is full of thrilling suspense.

In Sanskrit, at the beginning of the holy book, it cites some rituals to perform, which are described in the first part. Then the *Saptashati* begins. Each section of the book has a presiding deity. The first section is presided over by Shri Mahakali. The second section is presided over by Shri Mahalakshmi, and the third part is presided over by Shri Mahasaraswati. Each chapter is also connected to a deity, all of which are different forms of the Mother Goddess.

The Goddess appears when evil forces overcome the good forces, and, as a consequence, the world becomes powerless, succumbing to evil. At this point, the Mother Goddess is invoked, and She appears in multiple forms, slaying the opposing demonic forces. The Goddess is also connected to male Gods, for in the scriptures, every God has a consort (sometimes there are two or more.) Lakshmi is Vishnu's consort, Parvati is Shiva's, and Saraswati is Brahma's consort. They are all forms of the Mother Goddess, who is Mahalakshmi, Mahasaraswati, or Mahakali. The names may differ, but the Goddess is one and the same.

THE STORY OF SHRI LAKSHMI

Lakshmi is Vishnu's consort. Vishnu resides in Vaikuntha. Brahma is given the task of creation in the Holy Trinity, Shiva that of destruction, and Vishnu preserves the current state of existence. Vishnu is believed to rest in Kshirasagar or the Ocean of Milk. There, He lies on a serpent with one thousand heads. Lakshmi is awake, and She assists Her husband loyally.

It is said that when the divine beings churned the ocean, many jewels spilled out. Lakshmi was among them. The gems were to be equally divided, but the divine beings took all of them. Lakshmi emerged sitting on a lotus, and likewise, is often depicted as standing on a lotus. When Lakshmi appeared, all beings desired Her, but She had already made a decision. Lakshmi approached with a garland and placed it around Vishnu's neck. This is how She became Vishnu's divine consort.

Lakshmi has many other names. She is sometimes known as Padmavati, Kamala, Padmahasta, and Vishnupriya. At other times She is called Rama. Lakshmi is the Goddess of Wealth and Prosperity. She and Mahalakshmi are different. However, as the embodiment of the Mother Goddess, they are both the same.

Whenever Vishnu incarnates on the Earth, Lakshmi also incarnates. With Rama, She was Sita, and with Krishna, She was Rukmini. These two Gods are inseparable.

THE STORY OF SARASWATI

Saraswati was born to Brahma, the God of creation. Later, She became Brahma's wife. Because Brahma married his daughter, He is not worshiped. Saraswati is described as the Goddess of Learning and is honored in schools throughout India. She is depicted as sitting on a white lotus or swan, holding a book and a *veena*, which is a stringed musical instrument. She is also the Goddess of performing arts, especially classical music.

THE STORY OF PARVATI

Parvati is Shiva's second wife. Previously, Shiva was married to Sati, who was, in fact, an earlier incarnation of Parvati. The two Goddesses are the same.

Sati was a princess. Her father conducted a fire ritual and insulted Shiva by refusing to invite him. Out of anger towards Her father, Sati immolated herself and was later reborn as Parvati. The name Parvati refers to Her being a daughter of Himalaya (the mountain). The word *parvat* means mountain. Parvati is, therefore, a daughter of the mountain. She is also sometimes called Girija. When She came of age, Parvati did penance as she wanted to attract the attention of Shiva so that he would become Her husband. Shiva and Parvati have two sons, Kartikeya and Ganesh. Like Lakshmi, Parvati also has many other names, including Gauri, Uma, and Girija.

These three Goddesses, Lakshmi, Saraswati, and Parvati, are the consorts of the Holy Trinity.

*****

The Mother cult also encompasses *matrikas*, *yoginis*, and the worship of rivers. The river Ganga (Ganges), for example, originates from heaven. When Ganga descended from the celestial realm, Shiva offered the locks of his hair to assist with Her descent. Ganga is the most adored of the rivers. She is also the absolver of sins. She was brought in by Bhagiratha and is, therefore, called Bhagirathi at times. Ganga also appears as a character in the *Mahabharata*. Bhishma, one of the central characters, is Ganga's son. As for the other river Goddesses,

- Yamuna is the sister of Yama, the God of death. Lord Shri Krishna is associated with this river.

- Saraswati is a river that has vanished into thin air.

- Sindhu gave Her name to India.

- Narmada is the only river whose mere sight removes all sins.

- Kavery, Krishna, and Godavari are the South Indian rivers.

These rivers are worshiped literally. When referring to Ganga or Yamuna, the North Indians respectfully say Gangaji or Yamunaji.

In addition to the river Goddesses, there are water nymphs called *saat asara* who live in water.

There are also *yoginis*. They are sixty-four in number.

MOTHER WORSHIP IN OTHER COUNTRIES

The Babylonians worshiped the Mother in the form of two sisters. One was Ishtar, the bestower of life, and the other was Ereshkigal, the Goddess of Death who ended lives.

The Vikings worshiped Freya (or Freyja), the Goddess of Fertility. The day Friday is named after her.

The Roman Goddess Venus was also associated with fertility. Interestingly, Friday, the day named after Freya, is also regarded as sacred by worshipers of the Mother.

The Egyptians also praised the Mother Goddess in several forms. The most famous of these was Isis. Nut, the Goddess of the Sky, gave birth to divine beings. She closely resembles Aditi, the mother of the Gods in Hindu mythology.

The Sumerians worshiped Ninhusaga, Ninmah, Damgalnunna, Nintu, and Jammu. These Goddesses married male Gods and had a significant role to play whenever a crisis occurred.

Likewise, the Greeks worshiped Hera and Demeter, the Romans worshiped Tellus or Terra Mater (Mother Earth), the Aztecs worshiped Toci (Goddess of Purification, Healing, etc.), and the Yoruba religion worshiped Iansan and Oyas. In Christianity, Mary is revered as the mother of Jesus.

THE FIRST EPISODE

PRATHAM CHARITRA

I. THE KILLING OF MADHU AND KAITABHA

Salutations to Chandika

Markandeya said,

"I shall tell you about how the son of Sun God, the eighth Manu called Savarni, was born.

Listen to how Savarni became the master of Manvantara by the grace of Goddess Mahamaya.

In a Manvantara called Savarnik, there was a king named Surath in the Chaitra clan.

He cared for his subjects like a father, but then a Kolavidwansi king became his enemy.

Suratha fought a battle with him. Even though their army was not that strong, the enemy defeated him.

Harassed by the enemy, the king returned to his capital.

His ministers, who were very powerful and evil, exploited his wealth and his army.

Deserted by his people, the king rode his horse and proceeded towards the wild.

There he saw the hermitage of the sage Sumedha, which was full of tamed wild animals and the disciples of the sage.

He was enjoying the hospitality of the sage for a while by wandering hither and thither.

Then he thought about his capital and his subjects with love.

"My capital, well looked after by my ancestors, has become an orphan now without me. Those servants, and mine who have turned wicked, would they be looking after my city correctly?

What will happen to my pet elephant Sadamad (who is always under intoxication), who is now in the care of my enemy?

Those who have remained loyal might have received money and food and may have joined forces with my enemies.

The spendthrift ministers will also drain the coffers and my hard-earned resources very soon."

When the king was having such thoughts, he saw a merchant sitting there.

He asked that merchant, "Who are you? Why have you come to this hermitage? Why do you look so sad?"

When the merchant heard the kind words, he answered modestly,

"I am a merchant called Samadhi, born in a wealthy family. My children and wife have driven me out of my house because of greed.

My wife and children stripped my wealth from me, and my relatives have turned their back on me. I am miserable, so I have come to the forest.

Now I have no way of knowing what will happen to them.

Will they be all right?

What will happen to my sons? Would they follow the right path?"

The king said,

"Why do you have such tenderness for people who mistreated you out of greed?"

The merchant said humbly,

"What you say is true, but I cannot treat them with indifference. I am powerless in this regard.

I still care for those who abandoned me and cast aside their duties to their father and husband.

O King, I don't know the reason why I am still attached to those who have gone against me.

I still grieve for them, and because of this, I am troubled.

How can I describe my attachment to those who do not love me at all?"

Markandeya said,

"O Brahmin, then the king and the merchant named Samadhi, visited the sage Sumedha for an explanation.

They saluted the sage who instructed them to take their seats. They began talking to the sage,"

The king said,

"Lord, I need to ask you a question. Please answer this.

I don't have control over my thoughts, and it is causing me great misery.

Lord, I am deprived of my former kingdom, yet I am still emotionally attached to it. Why is that?

This merchant had been thrown out of his house by his sons, but he still loves them.

In some way, the merchant and I remain attached to those who have wronged us, and we know that this is not right.

Please tell us why we are tempted to do so, despite our awareness. Why have we lost our reason?"

The sage said,

"All animals know about this attachment. This attachment is present in all, in different degrees.

Some animals, like owls, are blind during daylight. Others, like sparrows and crows, are blind at night. And some animals, like tigers, cows, etc., have equal vision during both day and night.

Human beings are wise, but it is not true that they alone possess wisdom. All other beings such as animals, birds, and fish are also wise.

Human beings know what these other animals know. The knowledge of both is equal.

See how these birds feed their little ones when they are hungry?

Human beings love their children without any expectations. Don't you see that?

Despite this, even the wisest people are tempted by this attachment saying, 'this is mine, or it belongs to me.'

One should not be surprised by this. This grand illusion is a power of Vishnu called Yognidra. She tempts the whole universe.

Mahamaya attracts the minds of even the wise men and tempts them.

Mahamaya creates this visible and invisible universe. If She is pleased, she can give salvation to humanity.

Mahamaya can liberate us, and She is the supreme knowledge.

Because of Her, who is the might of God, we are attached to this world."

The king said,

"Lord, who is this Goddess you call Mahamaya? How was She born? What is Her function?

I want to know about Her nature and Her influence. I wish to learn everything from you."

The sage said,

"The Mother Goddess has always been there, but I shall tell you how She has expressed herself in different forms.

She appears for the deities, but She is beyond birth and death, so She is called Nitya (One Who is Always There.)

Long ago, the whole universe had been like a vast ocean, and after the affairs of the world were complete, the God Vishnu was exhausted and enjoyed his sleep.

Then two demons were born in the dirt that gathered in his ears. These two demons were named Madhu and Kaitabh.

They wanted something to eat, and they saw Brahmadeva sitting on the lotus that had emerged from the naval of Vishnu.

When he saw those horrific demons marching towards him, Brahmadeva was frightened. He was no match for those demons.

Vishnu was asleep, so he started praying to the Mother Goddess in the form of sleep. He prayed to the Goddess of the universe, the one who bears all the worlds, the Goddess of Sleep who is the glow of Vishnu."

Brahma said,

"O Goddess of Sleep, you are the basic sound. You are the sound uttered when fire offerings are made. You are the nectar in words. You are the three sounds.[2]

You are there in the unuttered sound. You are Sandhya[3] and Savitri. The three Vedas were born to you.

You give birth to this universe. You bear this universe. You nurture it, and finally, you destroy it.

In the beginning, you become the universe. When nurturing, you become the stability, and in the end, you become the destruction.

You are the great wisdom, the great illusion, great intelligence, and great memory. You become the great temptation, O great Goddess of the Goddesses.

You are the nature and the three qualities. You are the great stern night of time and temptation.

---

[2] Aim, Rheem, and Kleem.

[3] Literally translated as evening.

You are the wealth. You are Rheem. Intelligence and understanding are your symptoms. You are modesty, nourishment, satisfaction, peace, and contentment.

You have a sword in your hand (*Khadgini*) and a lasso (*Shulini*). You look terrifying (*Ghora*). You have a mace (*Gadini*) and a circular weapon (*Chakrini*). You have a conch (*Shankini*) and a bow (*Chapini*).

You are very beautiful, more beautiful than even the most beautiful. You are the greatest Goddess.

More than that, O Goddess occupying the whole universe, you are the power of the truth and untruth. How can I flatter you? It is beyond my ability.

How can I praise you who have made Shri Vishnu, the creator, preserver, and destroyer of this world, awaken? Who can?

You made Vishnu, I, and Mahadeva take form, so who has the power to praise you?

O Goddess, whom I praise thus, tempt these demons Madhu and Kaitabh with your power.

And awaken the master of this universe Shri Mahavishnu.

And motivate him to kill these demons."

The sage said,

"In this way, Brahmadeva praised the dark-natured Goddess for waking Vishnu and slaying the demons Madhu and Kaitabh.

Then the Goddess emerged from the ancient man's eyes, mouth, hands, heart, and chest to stand before Brahmadeva.

The master of this world, Shri Mahavishnu, awoke from his slumber atop the thousand-headed snake and saw the demons.

He stood up and fought, with his bare hands as his only weapon, for five thousand years.

Mahamaya tempted those two demons who had become overconfident about their might.

They said to Vishnu, "You ask for anything from us."

Bhagvan said,

"Both of you are pleased with me, so I ask that both of you should die at my hands.

I don't ask for anything else. I want only this."

The sage said,

"Thus deceived, the demons believed that the whole universe was full of water, so they said to the lotus-eyed Vishnu, "You should kill us at the place where there is no water."

The sage said,

"Vishnu agreed, and he put their heads on his thigh and killed them with his *chakra*.

In this way, the Goddess emerged and was praised by Brahmadeva himself. I shall tell you about Her other impact shortly."

Thus concludes the first chapter of the *Devi Mahatmya*, a part of Markandeya Purana's sub-chapter called *Savarnika Manvantara* (*The Times of Savarni Manu*).

This chapter is named *The Killing of Madhu and Kaitabha*.

Notes

This chapter is the first episode of the *Devi Mahatmya* concerning the emergence of the Mother Goddess. In Sanskrit, it is *Prathama Charitra*. When one recites the *Devi Mahatmya,* they read one *Charita* per sitting.

In this episode, we do not hear of any of the deeds of the Mother Goddess. The meaning of this episode is purely mystical. In it, God is sleeping after the creation of the world. There is no life anywhere.

The whole world is like a dormant ocean. Then two *asuras* (demons) are born from the dirt in the ears of God. Here, the story begins with the demons attempting to eat Brahmadeva, the creative form of the same God. The Creator is frightened, and He prays to the Mother Goddess in the form of sleep. This pleases the Mother Goddess, and She emerges from the body of the God. As a result, the God is then awakened. The Mother Goddess is everything. She induces the God to sleep, and only She has the power to awaken him.

The first chapter describes all of humanity. The king, the merchant, and the sage represent us. We have strong attachments towards the people who are very close and important to us. Even when they do not care for us, we cannot sever our relationships with them. These attachments act like bonds. These bonds are found in all animals. This is caused by the Great Mother, who is at the root of everything.

The king and the merchant belong to two different castes. The sage who is telling this belongs to another caste. As such, all the sections of society are represented since they all have to surrender to the Mother Goddess

The names which are used are also significant. The king is named Suratha, which means a "good chariot." The merchant is named Samadhi, which means a "trance-like mental state." One of the *asura* is called Madhu, which means honey, wine, or nectar.

Initially, the *asura* could not be defeated, but then the Mother Goddess tempted them, and they fell prey to the temptation, culminating in their death.

THE MIDDLE EPISODE

MADHYAM CHARITRA

II. THE DESTRUCTION OF MAHISHASURA'S ARMY

Om is for the welfare, and *Hreem* is the seed of Mahalakshmi.

The sage said,

"Earlier, the divine beings under the leadership of Indra fought a battle for one hundred years against the demons led by Mahishasura.

The demons defeated the divine beings, and after their defeat, Mahishasura assumed the role of Indra[4] and thus became the master of the heavens.

Then the defeated divine beings took Brahma, born from the lotus, and approached Shiva and Vishnu.

They described to Shiva and Vishnu the horrid exploits of Mahishasura and the dreadful defeat of the divine beings.

Mahishasura had assumed the rights of the Sun, the Moon, Yama (the God of Death), Varuna (the God of Water), and all other deities, and he was using them.

---

[4]   Ruler of the divine beings.

All the divine beings exiled from heaven by Mahishasura now roamed the Earth like mortal beings. They said,

"We have told you about the deeds of the enemy of the divine beings. We have come to you for help. How do we kill this demon?"

When Shiva and Vishnu heard this request, they became angry, and their eyebrows twisted in anger.

Then a fiery luster emerged from the angry mouths of Vishnu, Brahmadeva, and Shiva.

Another luster arose from the mouths of the other Gods, such as Indra, and combined with this blazing glow.

The flames of this light spread in all directions, and it resembled a flaming mountain to the Gods.

This fire from the Gods spread to all the three worlds and took on the form of a woman.

The fire from Shiva became Her face. The fire from Yama became Her hair, and the fire from Vishnu became Her biceps.

The fire from the Moon became Her breasts. The fire from Indra was Her midriff. The fire from Varuna became Her thighs and calves. The fire from the Earth turned into Her buttocks.

Brahma's fire became Her legs, and the fire from the Sun became Her fingers. The fire from Kubera was Her nose.

The fire from Prajapati turned into Her teeth. The flames of the Fire God turned into Her three eyes.

The Morning and Evening light made Her eyebrows, and the fire from Wind God made Her ears. The blazing light from all the Gods combined and thus made this Shivaa.

The Gods that Mahishasura had harassed were pleased to see this Goddess borne from the luster of the Gods.

All of the Gods presented their weapons to Her. Shiva, who carries a bow called Pinak, gave Her his trident.

Vishnu produced his circular weapon, the *chakra,* and gave it to Her. Varuna presented Her with his conch, and Agni, the Fire God, provided Her with his might.

The Wind God presented Her with a bow and two bags of arrows. The King of the Gods, Indra, offered Her his Vajra.

Indra also handed Her a bell from his elephant Airavat's neck. Yama gave Her one of his time bonds. Varuna gave Her a lasso.

Prajapati gave Her a rosary, and Brahmadeva gave Her his pot of water. The Sun God placed his rays in the roots of Her hair.

The God of Time gave Her a sword and shield. The Ocean of Milk presented Her with clothes woven of gold, which would never grow old, and a garland.

He also gave Her a jewel worn in a crest, earrings, bangles, and ornaments for Her arms.

He also gifted Her anklets, a necklace, and jeweled rings for Her fingers.

Vishwakarma (the carpenter God) gave Her Parashu (an axe-like weapon), various weapons, and impenetrable armor.

The Sea God gave Her two garlands of lotuses which would never wither, one to be worn on the head and one around the neck. He also presented Her with a beautiful lotus to hold in Her hand.

The Himalaya gave Her a lion as a vehicle and also different kinds of gems. Kubera gave Her a jug full of wine.

Shesha, who supports this Earth, offered Her a garland of snakes with jewels called Naghar.

After being provided with ornaments and arms by the Gods, the Goddess laughed with a menacing roar. Her terrifying laughter was heard again and again.

Her voice filled the sky with a dreadful echo.

The entire universe trembled, the storms covered the sea, and the Earth and mountains shook.

All the Gods hailed this Goddess seated on a lion, and the sages, humble with devotion, started praising Her.

When the demons saw how the universe was agitated, they became alert and prepared for battle.

"Ah, what is this?" said Mahishasura when he saw the Goddess surrounded by demons, and he leaped towards the sound of Her battle cries.

Mahishasura saw the Goddess who had filled the whole world with Her luster, who had shaken the world with Her footsteps, and whose crown had brightened the sky.

He saw the Goddess who had shaken the netherworld with the sound of Her bow and who had thousands of hands.

Then a battle commenced between the Goddess and the *asuras*. The conflict was so intense that it was visible from the sky in all directions.

The commander of Mahishasura, the great demon Chikshura, was engaged in combat. There was also another demon called Chamar, who was fighting with four divisions of the *asura* army.

Udagra was fighting with sixty thousand chariots, and Mahahanu was fighting with one *crore* chariots.

The demon Asiloma was fighting with five *crore* soldiers, and Bashkala was fighting with sixty *lakh* soldiers.

Ugradarshana, surrounded by one hundred *crore* chariots, was fighting with many elephants and horses.

Bidal, surrounded by five hundred *crore* chariots, was also fighting.

At the same time, tens of thousands of other demons with chariots, elephants, and horses were also attacking the Goddess.

Even Mahishasura was surrounded by a massive amount of chariots, elephants, horses, and soldiers.

They attacked the Goddess with *tomar*,[5] *bhindipal*, powerful weapons, sharp blades of grass, *parashu*,[6] and *pattish*.[7]

Some fought Her with lethal weapons or attempted to bind Her with lassoes. Others attacked Her with swords, intent on maiming the Goddess.

Then Chandika also used Her weapons and destroyed their weapons with ease.

The Goddess, praised by the Gods and the sages, was not affected and continued to use Her weapons.

Whenever the brave Goddess sighed, Her sighs were transformed into hundreds and thousands of soldiers.

Empowered by the blessings of the Goddess, they fought with *parashu*, *bhindipal*, sword, and *pettish*, destroying hundreds of demons.

---

[5] An iron club.

[6] A short javelin.

[7] Foot soldiers.

During the battle, the soldiers started beating drums and blowing conches.

The Goddess killed many demons with Her trident, mace, *rishti*,[8] and other weapons.

She slew the demons who had fainted due to the clamor of the bell. She bound others with Her lasso and dragged them across the battlefield.

Some were even split in two by Her sword, and others fell to the ground, injured by Her mace.

Other demons bled when She pierced them with the pointed grass. Those whom She pierced in the chest with Her trident collapsed, lifeless, to the ground.

There were arrows everywhere that hit all the *asuras*, who swiftly followed their path of their comrades into death.

Their hands were severed, throats slit, decapitated, and some even had their torsos sliced in half.

Other demons had their thighs slashed. Those that the Goddess had cleaved in half appeared to have only one arm, eye, or leg.

Decapitated demons rose from the ground, dancing to the tune of the war instruments.

The torsos picked up their heads or grew new ones. Still holding weapons in their hands, the demons pleaded to the Goddess, "Stop, stop."

---

[8] Bad luck or sword.

The corpses of elephants, horses, and lions were strewn all across the battlefield. Ruined chariots were lying beside them, abandoned.

A deep, tepid torrent of blood flowed from the carnage that had devastated the *asura* forces.

As fire can destroy vegetation and wood in a single moment, so had Ambika destroyed the legion of demons with ease and haste.

Her lion shook his mane, roaring fiercely, after slaughtering the demons.

The Goddess and Her allies were victorious and had conquered the *asura* army. In return, the Gods lavished them with flowers and praise.

Thus ends the second chapter of the *Devi Mahatmya* called *The Destruction of Mahishasura's Army.*

Notes

This is the second episode of the Mother's emergence. It is also known as the middle episode, as it is the second occasion when the Goddess has answered the God's prayers.

She appears whenever the evil powers are on the rise.

This time, She had to vanquish the demon Mahishasura, who had taken the form of a male buffalo. Mahisha means buffalo, an animal often used in farming. The buffalo is a beast of enormous strength. Perhaps this refers to ancient times when humans first learned agricultural skills and had attempted to domesticate wild buffalo. Women probably performed the early agricultural work and the domestication of farm animals.

All the names of the demons are symbolic. For example, Ugradarshana means 'One Whose Appearance is Fearsome.'

In this chapter, we learn how the Mother Goddess manifested. She is eternally present and is, therefore, also called Nitya. In the first chapter, the Goddess emanated from Vishnu's body. In this chapter, She takes form from the bodies of all the Gods. And every God bequeaths something to Her.

III. THE KILLING OF MAHISHASURA

The sage said,

"When the army of the demons was under attack, Chikshur, their commander, was so enraged that he came to fight the Goddess.

As a cloud rains on the peak of Mount Meru,[9] so too Chikshur showered arrows on the Goddess.

But the Goddess broke his arrows, slaying both his charioteer and horses with Her arrows.

She shattered the flag pole on his chariot and fired arrows at Chikshur when he broke his bow.

Then the demon, who had neither bow nor chariot, was forced to fight with only his sword and shield.

With his sword, Chikshur hit the lion's head and dexterously struck the arm of the Goddess.

But the sword broke when it came into contact with Her arm. Then Chikshur took his iron spike in his hands.

---

[9] A mythical mountain at the center of the world.

He threw the spike, which glistened like the sun, at the Goddess Bhadrakali.

When She saw the spike coming, the Goddess hurled Her own weapon, intercepting his spike. She then slew Chikshur, cutting his body into hundreds of pieces.

When their prestigious commander Chikshur was killed, Chamar, who was prosecuting the gods, came to battle Her astride an elephant.

He attacked the Goddess with all his power, but Ambika just said "*Hoom,*" and his attacks were aborted and rendered impotent.

When he saw his power defeated, the enraged demon Chamar threw his spike at the Goddess, which She destroyed with a volley of arrows.

Then the Goddess' lion leapt atop the elephant's head, attacking it valiantly.

Both the Goddess and the demon then dismounted and started fighting each other.

The lion pounced on the demon and, with a mere stroke of its paw, beheaded Chamar.

The Goddess threw rocks and trees at Udagra and killed him. She maimed Karal by striking him with the ivory pommel of Her sword.

The infuriated Goddess crushed Uddhata with Her mace, slew Bashkala with Her Bhindipal, and killed Tamra and Andhaka with Her bow.

The Parameshwari (Supreme Goddess) massacred Ugrasya, Ugravirya, Mahahanu, and Trinetra with Her trident.

She decapitated Bidala with Her sword and slew Durdhara and Durmukh with arrows.

When Mahishasura saw his army being destroyed, he assumed the form of a buffalo and began attacking the soldiers of the Goddess.

Mahishasura felled some with his kicks, others he struck with his tail, and some he impaled with his horns.

Many perished because of his speed. His howling slew some, while others died simply from the exhalation of Mahishasura.

After felling the army of the Goddess, when Mahishasura pounced on Goddess' lion, She became angry.

The demon also became enraged, and Mahishasura dug the Earth with his hooves, displacing mountains. Roaring proudly, Mahishasura aimed his horns towards the Goddess.

But because of his circular motions, the Earth had become very soft, and Mahishasura's tail aggravated the ocean.

When he attacked with his horns, the clouds broke into pieces. His breath caused the mountains to fall down onto the Earth with great force.

When She saw the powerful *asura* attacking Her allies, the Goddess was filled with rage, and She decided to kill him.

She threw Her lasso at Mahishasura and bound him, but the demon relinquished his buffalo form.

Mahishasura became a lion. Ambika attempted to behead him but then he changed from a lion into a man.

The Goddess shot him with Her arrows, but Mahishasura became a giant elephant.

That elephant then grabbed Her lion with his trunk, so the Goddess severed the elephant's trunk with Her sword.

Once again, the demon assumed the form of a buffalo, agitating the whole universe.

Then the furious Mother of the Universe, Chandika, began drinking wine and the red-eyed Goddess laughed.

The demon Mahishasura, possessed of great might and vigor, resumed his battle cries and hurled mountains at the Goddess.

She released Her arrows, and the mountains were destroyed. With Her face flushed from the wine, the Goddess said,

"Idiot, roar again and again till I finish my wine. Once I kill you, the Gods will shout with joy."

The sage said,

"Thus saying She pounced on Mahishasura and started whipping his stomach with Her lasso.

While She crushed him underfoot, She saw the demon emerge from the mouth of the buffalo; She stopped him with Her power.

Mahishasura was still struggling to exit the mouth of the buffalo when the Goddess decapitated him.

Witnessing the defeat of Mahishasura, the other demons fled, much to the delight of the Gods.

The Gods and the sages praised the Goddess, and the celestial dancers swayed to the songs of the Gandharvas.

Thus ends the chapter called T*he Killing of Mahishasura.*

Notes

The Goddess kills Mahishasura in this chapter. But is Mahishasura really a demon because he appears in various forms? Sometimes I feel that this is a battle similar to that which occurs every day in our body when microbes attack us, and the Mother is akin to our antibodies.

During one instance in this chapter, the Goddess is drinking wine. Madhu, however, has multiple meanings. Madhu can be honey or wine. However, She is definitely not drinking honey because Her eyes turn red as a result of intoxication. Moreover, this wine is given to Her by the Gods.

In the Vedas, there is also a description of the Gods becoming intoxicated from the consumption of Soma.

IV. THE PRAISE BY INDRA AND THE OTHER GODS

The sage said,

"When the Goddess killed the terrible demon and defeated his army, the Gods were very pleased.

 Bowing their heads and shoulders, they humbly saluted the Goddess and started praising Her with sweet words.

"We salute with devotion the Goddess Ambika who was born from the luster of the Gods, who has occupied this whole Earth, and who is adored by all Gods and sages.

We ask for Her blessings.

One whose incomparable influence and prowess are indescribable to Brahma, Vishnu, and Shiva, may Ambika give us the reason to nurture this universe and remove the fear of demons from our minds.

You who are Lakshmi in the homes of good people, Alakshmi[10] in the homes of evil people, the intelligence of wise people, the devotion of saintly people, and the humility of the high born, we salute thee.

---

[10]   The Goddess of Poverty.

Take care of this world.

O Goddess, how can we describe your incredible form or your valor in killing the demons or the different events in the war between gods and demons?

You are the primary cause of this world. You have three qualities, yet even Vishnu or Shiva could not fathom you.

You support this world, with a manifestation of one fraction of yourself because you are that supreme fundamental nature.

The word "*Swaha,*" which is uttered in the fire sacrifice and satiates the Gods, is you. The ancestors are satiated because of you. That is why they call you "Swadha."

You undertake different incredible observances, and you are the reason for salvation, so you are the science of Brahma.

Those who seek salvation control their bodily organs, free themselves of all vices, and meditate on you to understand the divine principle.

You are the Word. You are the essence of the three Vedas, the base of them, and the sound Om. You are the three Vedas who bless the three worlds, and you remove the problems of these worlds.[11]

---

[11] Vratya Vidhya.

You are Medha,[12] who understands all branches of learning. You live in the heart of the killer of Kaitabha, Vishnu, and are called Lakshmi.

You are Shiva's consort called Gauri, and as Durga, you help us cross this ocean of worldly life.

You have a slight smile on your face, which equals the full Moon, fresh and shining like gold. Despite that, Mahishasura attacked you, which is a wonder.

Your face is like the rising Moon, but when Mahishasura saw your eyebrows raised in fury, he didn't surrender, which is an even greater wonder. Who lives when confronting the God of death?

O Goddess, be pleased with us. If you are pleased in a particular way, you bless, and if you are angry, you destroy. We know this because you eliminated the colossal army of Mahishasura.

Whenever you bestow prosperity, you are pleased with devotees, who become famous in all the countries. Their wealth and fame continue increasing; their relatives are never sad and live their lives with loyal servants, sons, and wives.

When you bless them, these good beings continue to perform their duties as given in the scriptures and finally reach heaven. In this world and the other world, you are the one who provides the best rewards.[13]

---

[12] Supreme intelligence.

[13] Fruits of action – *phalam.*

Even if somebody remembers you unknowingly, you remove his or her fear, and if somebody remembers you consciously, you bestow him with the intelligence to prosper. Who can be kinder than you who bless all, O remover of poverty, sorrow, and fear?

Now that the demons have been slain let the world be pleased. They may have committed evil deeds and are now condemned to hell, but they died fighting on the battlefield, so you give them a great afterlife in heaven.

Could you not burn them to ash just by a glance? Why did you kill them with your weapons? Because you feel that those demons, sanctified by your weapons, should go to heaven.

The demons were not affected by the luster of your sword, or the glow of your spike, because they were looking at your beautiful face, which shone like a rising moon.

You possess a nature that removes the destructive tendencies in bad people.

Your incredible beauty, your courage in killing those demons who had beaten the divine beings is excellent, and yet you remain sympathetic towards the enemy.

O benevolent Goddess, how can we compare to your valor? Where can we behold such incomparable beauty that is fearsome to the enemy?

You possess sternness in battle and kindness of heart, the two opposing qualities in you.

We salute you, you who protected the three worlds by defeating the *asuras*. You sent them to heaven and removed the fear from our minds.

Protect us with your spike, protect us with your sword, protect us with the noise of your bell, and the sound of your bow.

O Chandika, move your spike to the east, to the west, and protect us. Move your spike to the south and the north and protect us, O Ishwari.

Your various forms, some of which are mild while others are fierce, will protect us and the three worlds.

Ambika, protect us from all sides with your sword, mace, and spike held in your tender hands."

The sage said,

"In this way, the divine beings praised the Goddess, the Mother of the universe, and worshiped Her with sacred flowers from heaven and incense.

After burning the incense, they stood humbly before the Goddess who spoke pleasantly to them,

"O Gods, you can ask for anything from me."

The divine beings answered,

"Bhagvati, you have done everything for us. Nothing has been spared. You have destroyed our greatest enemy, Mahishasura.

If you wish to give us a boon, then promise us that you will appear and solve our problems whenever we remember you.

And O Goddess with a lovely face, whoever worships you with these words, will be blessed by you with wealth, prosperity, and welfare; it will increase every year as you have blessed us."

The sage said,

"O King, the Goddess who had appeared because of their prayers, said, "So be it" and disappeared.

O King, I have told you how the Goddess who made the three worlds happy emerged from the bodies of the divine beings.

Again, She emerged from the body of Gauri to defeat Shumbha and Nishumbha.

I shall tell you how the Goddess, favoring the divine beings and protecting the three worlds, emerged. Listen to this."

Thus ends the fourth chapter of the *Devi Mahatmya* called *Praise by Indra and the Other Gods.*

Notes

The praise of the Gods is regarded as being very powerful. If one recites this regularly, the Mother Goddess is pleased, and She takes care of Her devotee.

The original Sanskrit mantras are extraordinarily potent and possess an excellent rhythmic pattern. In terms of poetic composition, they are also highly formidable.

However, I believe that if one has devotion and faith in his or her heart and prays to the Goddess in any language, She will answer that prayer.

THE BEST EPISODE

UTTAM CHARITRA

V. THE CONVERSATION BETWEEN THE GODDESS AND THE AMBASSADOR

Om is the seed of welfare, and *Cleem* is the seed of Mahasaraswati.

The sage said,

"Earlier, the *asuras* Shumbha, Nishumbha, and their powerful army usurped a portion of the fire sacrifice which belonged to Indra and the other Gods

These two demons began to perform the duties of the Sun, the Moon, Kubera,[14] Yama,[15] and Varuna[16] in their own way.

They enjoyed the wealth of the Wind God and the Fire God. All the defeated Gods were exiled from their thrones and heaven.

Then those Gods whose rights had been usurped by the two *asuras* remembered the undefeated Goddess,

---

[14] Treasurer of the Gods.

[15] The God of Death.

[16] The God of the Element Water.

"She has promised us that whenever we remember Her, She would solve all our problems."

Thinking about this, all the Gods went to the great mountain Himalaya, and started praying to Vishnumaya devotedly.

The Gods said,

"We salute the Goddess. We salute Mahadevi. We salute Shivā.[17] We salute Bhadra. Humbly, we pay our obeisance.

We salute Raudra.[18] We salute Nitya, Gauri, and Dhatri again and again. We eternally salute Jyotsna, Indurupini,[19] and Sukha.[20]

We are humble before Kalyani.[21] We bow again and again before the wealth-giving Vruddhi,[22] boon-giving Siddhi,[23] and Kurmi.[24] We salute you in the form of Nairuti, Rajlakshmi, and Sharvani.

---

[17] The feminine form of Shiva.

[18] The feminine aspect of Rudra, the Vedic form of Shiva.

[19] Indu means Moon and Indurupini means one who has the 'Beauty of the Moon.'

[20] Sukha means happiness.

[21] One Who Brings Welfare.

[22] Growth.

[23] Fulfillment.

[24] The female form of Kurma – the tortoise which is the second incarnation of Lord Vishnu.

Again and again salutations to Durga, Durgpara, Sara, Sarvakarini, Khyati, Krishna, and Dhumra.

We bow before the very beautiful Saumya[25] and the terrible Atiraudra. We salute these forms. We salute again and again to Jagatpratistha and Krutadevi.

Three salutes to the Goddess who is in all beings and is called Vishnumaya.

Three salutes the Goddess who is in all beings as vitality (*Chetna*).

Three salutes to the Goddess who is in all beings as intelligence (*Buddhi*).

Three salutes to the Goddess who is in all beings as sleep (*Nidra*).

Three salutes to the Goddess who is in all beings as hunger (*Kshudha*).

Three salutes to the Goddess who is in all beings as Shadow (*Chaya*).

Three salutes to the Goddess who is in all beings as Power (*Shakti*).

Three salutes to the Goddess who is in all beings as thirst (*Trushna*).

Three salutes to the Goddess who is in all beings as forgiveness (*Kshama*).

---

[25] Moderate.

Three salutes to the Goddess who is in all beings as caste (*Jaati*).

Three salutes to the Goddess who is in all beings as blushing (*Lajja*).

Three salutes to the Goddess who is in all beings as peace (*Shanti*).

Three salutes to the Goddess who is in all beings as implicit faith (*Shraddha*).

Three salutes to the Goddess who is in all beings as luster (*Kanti*).

Three salutes to the Goddess who is in all beings as wealth (*Lakshmi*).

Three salutes to the Goddess who is in all beings as a quality of mind (*Vrutti*).

Three salutes to the Goddess who is in all beings as memory (*Smruti*).

Three salutes to the Goddess who is in all beings as compassion (*Daya*).

Three salutes to the Goddess who is in all beings as contentment (*Tushti*).

Three salutes to the Goddess who is in all beings as mother (*Matru*).

Three salutes to the Goddess who is in all beings as illusion (*Bhranti*).

We salute the Goddess who is at the base of all beings' organs and who has occupied all beings.

Three salutes to the Goddess who has occupied the whole universe as the life force,

The benevolent Ishwari, whom we had prayed to with Indra and served every day for our cause, shall bless us and remove all our problems.

Now, harassed by the evil and formidable *asura*, we worship the power of the Goddess, who, as we have remembered, shall destroy all of our problems instantly."

The sage said,

"O Prince, when the divine beings were praising and praying, Parvati came there to bathe in the Ganga river.

This alluring woman with glorious eyes and beautiful eyebrows said to the divine beings, "Who are you praying to?" Then the Goddess Shivā, who had emerged from the body of Parvati, said to Her,

"These divine beings, defeated in battle by Shumbha and banished from heaven by Nishumbha, are praying to me."

After this, Ambika emerged from the bodily cocoon of Parvati, and She was called Kaushiki.[26]

---

[26] *Kosha* means cocoon.

Parvati told Kaushiki what to do and departed. After Her departure, Parvati (Kaushiki) became black in color and started living in the Himalayas as Kalika.

Then Shumbha and Nishumbha's servants, Chanda and Munda, saw that Ambika or Kaushiki now had an exquisite form.

The pair told Shumbha, "Lord, there is an extremely beautiful lady who is brightening Himalaya with Her beauty.

O King of Demons, we haven't seen anybody prettier than Her. Know that she must be a divine lady and possess Her.

That woman who is brightening all the directions is a jewel among females, so, O King of Demons, you must take a look at Her.

Lord, you have a fine elephant, a fine horse, and jewels from the three worlds that increase the splendor of your house.

You took from Indra the elephant Airavata, Uchaishrawa the horse, and Parijata the divine fragrant tree.

You have an incredible chariot adorned with the finest gems drawn by swans that previously belonged to Brahmadeva; this is now in your custody.

You took from Kubera endless treasure, and the ocean gave you a garland which never withers.

You took Varuna's umbrella and its golden rain. The great chariot of Prajapati is in your house.

Yama's mighty weapon, Utkrantida, was taken from him by you. Varuna's lasso is with your brother.

Whatever gems are created by the ocean are with Nishumbha. The God of Fire gave you two fine robes purified in flame.

You have obtained all these jewels, so why do you not possess this fine jewel among women?"

The sage said,

"When Shumbha heard this from Chanda and Munda, he sent a great demon called Sugriva as his ambassador to the Goddess saying,

"You tell Her these things and convince Her in such a way that makes Her come to me voluntarily. I command you to do this as soon as possible."

The ambassador went to the majestic Himalaya where the Goddess was sitting and talked to Her in a sweet and soft voice.

The ambassador said,

"O Goddess, the King of Demons, Shumbha, is the greatest one alive in all the three worlds. He has sent me as his ambassador.

He has conquered all his enemies, so his word is the last even in the divine worlds. Listen to what he has said.

"All the three worlds belong to me. All the Gods are under my command. I take the offerings from the fire sacrifice in different forms.

All the best jewels in the three worlds are in my custody. I have taken away Indra's vehicle, the jewel among elephants called Airawata.

When the Ocean of Milk was churned, a jewel among horses called Uchaishrawa appeared, which the Gods have dedicated to me humbly.

O Goddess, the jewels of the Gods, Yakshas, and Nagas are now mine.

We regard you as a jewel among women, so please come to us because we adore jewels.

O Goddess who glances, accept my great valiant younger brother Nishumbha or me because you are a jewel among women.

If you accept me, you will accept immense wealth. Consider this carefully and accept me."

The sage said,

"When the ambassador said all this, the benevolent Goddess Durga, who bears these worlds, smiled to Herself and said seriously,"

"You speak the truth. You do not lie. Shumbha is the master of the three worlds. Nishumbha is also great.

But in this matter, I have taken an oath. How can I go back on that? Listen to the promise I made with little thought.

Only the one who defeats me in battle can destroy my pride, and the one who is equal to me in prowess will become my husband.

So let the great demon Shumbha or Nishumbha come here, defeat me, and take my hand in marriage. Why should there be any delay?"

The ambassador said,

"You have become arrogant. You should not speak to me like this. Who in all the three words could possibly confront Shumbha or Nishumbha?

Even the Gods cannot equal these *asuras* in battle. How could a lone woman like you stand against them?

How can you, a single woman, face Shumbha and other demons whom even Indra failed to defeat?

In my opinion, you should go to Shumbha and Nishumbha peacefully. Otherwise, they will drag you to them by your hair, which is undignified."

The Goddess said,

"You are correct. Shumbha is very powerful, and Nishumbha is equally bold. But what should I do? I made this oath earlier without paying heed to the consequences.

So, go and humbly convey my words to the master of the *asuras*. Let him decide the appropriate course of action."

Thus ends the fifth chapter of the *Devi Mahatmya* called *The Conversation Between the Goddess and the Ambassador.*

Notes

In this chapter, the Goddess emerges from the body of Parvati, who is Shiva's eternal consort. The *asuras* are Shumbha and Nishumbha. The patterns seen here are similar to those previously conveyed. The Gods have been defeated, and demons have usurped their rights.

Here the Goddess is described as being exceptionally beautiful. She is also described as being a jewel among women.

In the dialogue between the Goddess and the ambassador, the dialog is clever, especially when the ambassador tries to convince the Mother to come with him.

VI. THE KILLING OF DHUMRALOCHANA

The sage said,

"When the ambassador heard this, he became furious and went to the King of Demons to relay the message in detail.

After listening to the ambassador, the King of Demons became furious and spoke to Dhumralochana, the commander of the demon army.

"Dhumralochana, go with your army and bring me that awful woman. Make Her writhe in pain and drag Her to me by Her hair.

If anybody comes to protect Her, kill him without giving a thought to who he is. He might be a God, Yaksha, or Gandharva."

The Sage said,

"By order of the King, Dhumralochana immediately went back to Her with an army of sixty thousand demons.

He saw the Goddess resting on the Himalaya and shouted, "Come to Shumbha and Nishumbha quickly.

If you do not come voluntarily, I shall drag you forcefully by the hair, causing you great pain."

The Goddess said,

"The King of Demons has sent you. You are strong and are surrounded by an army. If you are taking me forcefully, what can I do?"

The sage said,

"When She said this, Dhumralochana pounced on Her, but the Goddess burnt him to ashes with the sound *hoom*.

The demon army immediately started attacking Ambika by bombarding Her with sharp arrows, weapons, and *parashu*.

Then the vehicle of the Goddess, Her fierce lion, roared loudly and shook his mane. He assaulted the demons.

He slew some demons with his claws and his mighty teeth; others he crushed with pure strength.

He disemboweled them with his talons and beheaded others with his jaws.

He severed the limbs of others and then, shifting his mane, drank the blood of the dead.

That great lion, the vehicle of the Goddess, easily defeated the army of demons.

When he heard that the Goddess had killed Dhumralochana and Her lion had destroyed his army, the King of Demons became furious.

His lips quivered with rage as he issued orders to the demons, Chanda and Munda.

"Chanda, Munda, raise a massive army and bring that woman to me immediately.

Drag Her by Her hair, bind Her, and bring Her to me. If anything suspicious occurs, kill Her with your weapons.

Kill that awful woman and Her lion or capture Ambika and bring Her here."

Thus ends the sixth Chapter of *Devi Mahatmya* called *The Killing of Dhumralochana*.

Notes

In this chapter, the demon's name is Dhumralochana. *Dhumra* means smoke, and *lochan* means eyes. Therefore, the demon has eyes like smoke. Does this symbolize extinguishing the fire by blowing? This chapter hints at some of the things the Goddess does.

Moreover, the demon is killed simply by uttering the sound "*hoom*."

Hoom is a sacred word. It is said that the Mother Goddess resides in this sound. Interestingly enough, this sound is also considered to be holy in other religions.

VII. THE KILLING OF CHANDA AND MUNDA

The sage said,

"Thus ordered by Shumbha, the demon army with four divisions, led by Chanda and Munda, proceeded forth to capture the Goddess.

They saw the Goddess atop the golden peaks of Himalaya, riding the lion with a smile on Her face.

When they saw Her, the arrogant demons raised their swords and other weapons. Some even approached and tried to seize her.

Then Ambika became furious. Anger blackened Her face.

From Her forehead emerged the wrathful Kali, holding a sword and a lasso in Her hands.

She held a staff in one hand with a human head upon it. She wore a garland of human skulls around Her neck. Her countenance was intense because the flesh of Her body was withered and desiccated.

Her mouth was wide open, and Her protruding tongue made Her frightening to behold. Her eyes were bloodshot, and Her terrifying shrieks echoed from all directions.

Arriving thus, She proceeded to slaughter the demons and started devouring their army.

She lifted the elephants with the *mahouts* on them, the bells, and the back guards, and put them in Her mouth.

She lifted the chariots with horses, charioteers, and the warriors and put them in Her mouth, grinding them viciously between Her teeth.

She dragged some demons by the hair and others by the neck. She kicked some to death and others She killed with Her arms.

Whenever arrows were shot at Her, She devoured these also and angrily broke them.

She destroyed the entire army of the *asuras*. She swallowed some and maimed many.

Some perished by the sword, some by the *khatwanga*,[27] and others died because of Her sharp teeth.

When he saw the demon army rapidly annihilated, Chanda arrived to engage in battle with Kali.

He launched many arrows and circular weapons at Kali and literally eclipsed Her.

---

[27] A long studded club.

Then dreadful Kali opened Her horrifying maw. She howled loudly and laughed at Chanda.

Kali took Her great sword and pounced on Chanda, grasping him by the hair as She proceeded to behead him.

When Munda saw Chanda dying, he came to combat Kali, but she lifted Her blade and decapitated Munda also.

When they saw that Chanda and Munda had been slaughtered, the remaining demons became frightened and fled the battlefield in all directions.

Then Kali, holding the heads of Chanda and Munda in Her hands, went to Chandika. With a thundering laugh, She said,

"In this fire sacrifice of battle, I killed these two beasts and have brought them to you as a present. You will kill Shumbha and Nishumbha yourselves."

The sage said,

"When She saw the heads of Chanda and Munda in Her hands, that benevolent Chandika said to Kali in a sweet voice,

"O Goddess, as you have come with the heads of Chanda and Munda, *you will be famous in this world as Chamunda.*"

Thus ends the seventh chapter of the *Devi Mahatmya* called *The Killing of Chanda and Munda.*

Notes

This chapter informs us of the emergence and nature of Kali. She is an aggressive form of the Goddess. Kali wears a garland of skulls and is usually depicted with a protruding tongue. Shri Ramkrishna Paramhansa worshiped Her at Dakshineshwar temple. Kali appeared before him and spoke to him.

Kali is a kindhearted Mother, even though Her external appearance is fearsome. Kali is also known as Bhadrakali. Here *bhadra* means good. She is also called Mahakali.

This chapter describes Kali as emerging from the forehead of Ambika. She is the same Goddess.

The Goddess only appears in Her wrathful form to demons and people who possess a malevolent character.

VIII. THE KILLING OF RAKTABIJA

The sage said,

"After the death of Chanda and Munda, following the destruction of the demonic army, the King of the Demons became furious.

Because of his rage, the great Shumbha was not in control of his senses, and he ordered all the commanders to ready their armies.

The eighty-six commanders and the cunning eighty commanders of Kambu and their armies proceeded to the battleground.

The fifty clans of Kotivirya demons and fifty clans of Dhaumra were also instructed to proceed.

"I order Kalak, Daurhad, Maurya, and Kalkeya to be ready and proceed."

Shumba, the stern ruler of the demons, then set forth with an army of thousands of demons.

When Chandika saw that terrible army marching toward Her, She raised Her bow, and the great sound of the bow filled the vacuum between the Earth and the sky.

O King, then the lion roared, and Ambika increased its intensity with the sound of Her bell.

The shrieks of Kali, who had opened Her mouth wide was even more tremendous than the sound of the bow, lion, and bell.

After hearing that noise, the demons became enraged and surrounded Chandika, the lion, and Kali from all sides.

O King, then to kill the enemies of Gods and provide welfare for the Gods, the female forms of the Gods emerged.

From the bodies of Brahmadeva, Shiva, Kartikeya, Vishnu, and Indra, the Goddesses emerged and approached Chandika.

These new female powers had a similar appearance, ornaments, and vehicles to the male Gods and were ready to combat the *asuras*.

First came a Goddess with a rosary and the *pooja* pot.[28] Riding a flying chariot drawn by swans, She is known as Brahmani.

Riding on a bull with a trident in one hand and another hand raised in blessing, Maheshwari appeared, wearing bangles of great snakes and a crescent moon atop Her head.

---

[28] This is called *kamandalu*. For monks it is a multipurpose pot.

Wielding a powerful weapon, Kaumari appeared as the female form of Kartikeya, astride a peacock.

Vaishnavi appeared, riding on an eagle, holding a conch, mace, *chakra*, and a sword. Vishnu's shakti, the incomparable form of the boar of fire sacrifice, arrived as the Goddess Varahi.

The half-lion and half-human Narsinhi arrived tousling her fur like constellations of stars.

Holding the Vajra and seated on an elephant, Aindri also arrived. Like Indra, She, too, had a thousand eyes.

Surrounded by the *shakti* of the gods, Shiva said to Chandika, "For the sake of my love, slay these demons."

Then another female form emerged from the body of the Goddess, who growled like a hundred jackals.

And that undefeatable Goddess with gray locks said to Shiva, "O Lord, you go to Shumbha and Nishumbha as my ambassador.

Tell the arrogant Shumbha, Nishumbha, and the other war-mongering demons to let Indra become the master of the three worlds.

Let the Gods receive their offerings from the fire sacrifice. If you want to stay alive, go to the netherworld.

If idiotically, you still desire combat and foolishly take pride in your military prowess, then do come to me, and let my jackals draw contentment from devouring your flesh."

As the Goddess appointed Shiva as Her ambassador, she became famous as "Shivaduti."[29]

When the demons heard the message from the Goddess that Shiva relayed, they were outraged and went to the place where Katyayani was standing.

They shot arrows at Her and attacked the Goddess with swords.

She drew Her bow in return and destroyed all their weapons.

Kali went ahead and roamed the battleground, wounding the enemies with Her trident and *khatwang*.

Brahmani sprinkled water from Her *pooja* pot and disabled Her foes.

Aindri killed many with Her *vajra*, and the demons fell to the ground with blood flowing from their bodies.

Varahi attacked them with Her teeth and Her *chakra*, disemboweling Her opponents.

Narsinhi, who was stunning the world with Her roars, eviscerated the demons with Her claws and stalked the battleground devouring them.

The terrifying laughter of Shivduti horrified the demons so much that they fainted, and She consumed their bodies.

---

[29] *Duta* means ambassador.

The soldiers of the Mother Goddess were furious, and they pursued the demons as they attempted to escape the wrath of the Goddess.

Raktabija, a powerful demon, saw the other demons fleeing the battlefield and came to fight.

Whenever any drop of blood fell from his body onto the Earth, another demon emerged from it.

When he was fighting Aindri with his mace, She struck Raktabija with Her *vajra*.

This wound made Raktabija bleed profusely. Each drop of blood gave birth to a new demon that was as strong as Raktabija himself.

These newborn demons readied their weapons to fight the army of the Mother Goddess.

Aindri struck Raktabija again, crushing his skull this time. Thousands of new warriors emerged from the blood.

Vaishnavi also wounded Raktabija with Her *chakra* and mace. Her *Chakra* also pierced Raktabija, and so many demons were born from his blood.

Kaumari hit Raktabija with Her most potent weapon, Varahi struck him with Her sword, and Maheshwari impaled him with Her trident.

Raktabija, born in a Diti clan, was now also enraged and began to strike the various forms of the Mother Goddess with his mace.

Whenever a weapon hit him, torrents of Raktabija's blood would flow like a river, from which thousands of new demons were formed.

The demons born from Raktabija blood now covered the entire Earth, and the divine beings became frightened.

Chandika, when She saw the apprehension of the Gods, laughed and spoke to Kali, "Chamunda, open your mouth wide.

Whenever I wound Raktabija, you must quickly drink his blood. Do not let it fall on the Earth.

Then devour all the other demons on the battlefield.

Once Raktabija's blood has been drained completely, he will perish, and the war will end.

No more demons will emerge."

The Goddess then struck Raktabija with Her lasso.

Kali started drinking his blood.

With great agility, the demon struck Chandika with his mace, but Chandika was not injured.

Blood gushed from Raktabija's body like a fountain, which Chamunda drank with Her mouth.

More demons were born from that blood in Chamunda's mouth, but She simply swallowed and consumed them, along with Raktabija's blood.

Then Kaushiki attacked Raktabija, whose blood was still being devoured by Chamunda, with Her lasso, sword, arrows, *vajra,* and *rusti.*

When he had been completely drained of blood, all these weapons struck the mighty demon Raktabija as he fell to the ground.

Then, O King, the Gods were pleased, and the various female manifestations of the Gods danced, intoxicated with Raktabija's blood."

Thus ends the eighth chapter of the *Devi Mahatmya* called *The Killing of Raktabija.*

Notes

This chapter explains the emergence of the various forms of the Goddess, which are all aspects of Mother Goddess worship. It illustrates how people perceived different deities and the feminine forms of the male Gods. It is an attempt to merge all cults into a similar belief system.

The central figure is Shiva. Therefore, worship of the Goddess was probably a development of the existing Shaivite sect. Interestingly, Shiva's son Skanda or Kumara is mentioned, but Ganapati, his second son, is not. Kaumari is the female form of Kumara, whose vehicle is a peacock. Therefore, the *Devi Mahatmya* may predate the Ganapati cult, also known as Ganapatya, as the text contains no mention of Ganapati.

The story of Raktabija is as intriguing as his name is revealing. *Rakta* means blood, and *bija* means seed. The name Raktabija means the *source of blood*. Each drop of blood enables him to multiply, creating copies of himself. This could be a reference to micro-bacteria, which can quickly multiply from a single source into millions.

IX. THE KILLING OF NISHUMBHA

The king said,

"Lord, you told me the incredible tale of the Goddess in which She killed Raktabija.

I want to know about the trouble caused by Shumbha and Nishumbha after the fall of Raktabija."

The sage said,

"After the fall of Raktabija and the death of many demons, Shumbha and Nishumbha became extremely angry.

Watching his powerful army being annihilated, the frenzied Nishumbha bit his lips in rage and rushed forward to kill the Goddess with his forces.

The demons who were in the front, back, and both sides angrily surrounded the Goddess, gritting their teeth as they prepared to slay Her.

Even the valiant Shumbha, with his mighty army, fought with the other forms of the Goddess and came to murder Chandika in anger.

They fired arrows at the Goddess, and in return, the Goddess showered arrows on them.

It was like two clouds raining on the Earth. Such was the scope of the war between them.

Chandika quickly destroyed their arrows, but Her weapons wounded the demons.

Nishumbha, with a shield in one hand and his sword held high, struck the lion, the vehicle of the Goddess, on his head.

When She saw Her lion wounded, the Goddess attacked and broke both the sword of Nishumbha and his crescent-shaped shield.

After his shield and sword were smashed, Nishumbha threw another powerful weapon at the Goddess, which She cleaved in two with Her *chakra*.

Nishumbha became furious and reached for his lasso, but the Goddess punched him and destroyed it.

Then he threw his mace at the Goddess, but She destroyed it with Her trident.

When Nishumbha advanced on the Goddess, with an axe in his hand, the Goddess felled him by releasing a volley of arrows.

Watching his valiant brother falling unconscious on the ground, the enraged Shumbha appeared, intent on killing the Goddess.

He was standing in his chariot and he raised his eight arms, all holding weapons, so that they filled the whole sky.

When the Goddess saw him coming, She blew Her conch and made a loud unbearable noise.

Then She rang Her bell, filling all the directions with its sound, eclipsing the army of demons.

Her lion roared wildly, and its howling filled the air, frightening everything.

Kali raised Herself to the sky and beat the Earth with both Her hands. The noise engulfed all other sounds.

Shivduti laughed excitedly, and the demons lost their nerves. Shumbha became extremely angry.

When Ambika said, "Stop, stop, O wicked one," the divine beings in the sky shouted, "Victory to thee."

Shumbha came forward and threw a potent weapon, blazing with fire.

When the flames rose, the Goddess threw meteors on it and extinguished the burning weapon.

Then Shumbha roared like a beast and stunned the three worlds. The echoes of this noise dwarfed all other sounds.

Hundreds of the Goddess's arrows were destroyed by Shumbha, and She, in turn, destroyed hundreds of Shumbha's arrows.

Angrily, the Goddess struck Shumba with Her spike and wounded him. Shumbha lost consciousness and collapsed to the ground.

But then Nishumbha regained his senses and readied his bow to fire at the Goddess, Kali, and the lion.

The son of Danu, master of the demons, raised his ten thousand hands bearing weapons and overshadowed Chandika with his blades.

The Goddess Durga, the annihilator of the demon Durgasura, became furious. She released Her arrows and destroyed Nishumbha's weapons.

Then Nishumbha rushed forward, brandishing his mace, intent on killing Chandika.

Chandika destroyed his mace with her sword. Then he raised his spike.

Nishumbha, who had beaten the divine beings, rushed forward with his spike. Chandika pierced his heart with Her weapon.

Another powerful demon began to emerge from the wound and said: "Stop."

With a mocking laugh, the Goddess decapitated the demon. Then Nishumbha fell to the ground.

The remaining demons had their throats slit by the claws of the lion or were eaten by Kali and Shivduti.

Kaumari sliced the demons to pieces, and Brahmani sprinkled Her water, which made the demons flee.

Other demons collapsed, maimed by Maheshwari's trident. Varahi also hit many and slew them.

Vaishnavi killed some with Her *chakra,* while Aidri killed others with her *vajra*.

Many demons died. Some also fled, and any remaining demons were devoured by Kali, Shivduti, and the lion king.

Thus ends the ninth chapter of the *Devi Mahatmya* called *The Killing of Nishumbha.*

Notes

The evil demon Nishumbha is killed by the Goddess in this chapter. Interestingly, when Nishumbha is slain, another demon emerges from his body and tells the Goddess to "stop." Was the body of the demonic Nishumbha like a robot, with another demon inside it controlling the body?

Both this chapter and the next one read like science fiction.

X. THE KILLING OF SHUMBHA

The sage said,

"Watching his dear brother die and the army's massacre, Shumbha who was regaining consciousness, muttered angrily,

"Durga, you are so proud of your little might. You should not feel proud. You are fighting through the strength of others."

The Goddess said,

"O wicked one. I am unique in this world. There is no one like me. Watch these forms of mine as they merge into me."

Then all the Goddesses, led by Brahmani, joined with the body of the Goddess, and only Ambika was visible.

The Goddess said,

"With my influence, I was standing here in many forms. Now, I have finished it. I am alone in this battle, so take heed."

The sage said,

"Then a war broke out between the Goddess and Shumbha, which was observed by both the divine beings and the demons.

The deluge of arrows, sharp blades, and frightening missiles stunned all who watched the dreadful battle as the war between the Goddess and Shumbha escalated.

Ambika hurled hundreds of divine weapons, but the demon destroyed them all with equally strong weapons.

And any weapons he used were quickly destroyed by Parameshwari when She uttered "*Hoom.*"

The demon surrounded the Goddess with hundreds of arrows, and the agitated Goddess destroyed his bow with Her arrows.

The demon held a powerful missile in his hands, but the Goddess destroyed it with her *chakra.*

Then the demon took a sword and a shield, decorated with hundreds of lunar symbols, and attacked the Goddess.

As Shumbha strode toward her, Chandika shot her arrows and tore his sword and shield to pieces.

She also killed the horses with the charioteer.

After the horses and the charioteer were slain, Shumbha took a giant *mudgar*[30] in his hands.

---

[30] A type of club.

But as he was pouncing, the Goddess destroyed his *mudgar*. Despite this, the demon pounced on Her with a raised fist and punched the Goddess's chest.

In retaliation, the Goddess hit him with Her palm.

The blow from Her palm made Shumbha stagger, but he quickly regained his footing.

He grabbed the Goddess and flew high into the sky. Chandika now had to fight him without any support.

The sages ceaselessly watched as the Goddess grappled with the demon.

After wrestling with Shumbha for a long time, She lifted him, spun him in circles, and then threw his body down.

The fiendish Shumbha stood up after his fall and lunged at the Goddess, with his fists raised and ready to kill Her.

But the Goddess impaled Shumbha with Her spike, and dying, he collapsed on the ground.

Wounded by the edge of the blade, the demon's corpse fell to the Earth. The impact of his body's landing shook all the islands and mountains.

When the vile Shumbha perished, the whole universe was pleased and became content. Even the sky became clear.

After his death, the meteoric clouds which bestowed ill omens earlier were soothed, and the rivers started to flow normally once more.

Thus, after the fall of Shumbha, the hearts of the divine beings were delighted, and the Gandharvas began to sing sweetly.

Others also commenced playing musical instruments. The Apsaras danced, and the Sun took on a special glow.

Thus ends the tenth chapter of the *Devi Mahatmya* called *The Killing of Shumbha*.

Notes

Shumbha was undoubtedly a mighty warrior. He was almost equal to the Goddess in power, but when evil and good forces come into conflict, the good always prevails. Once Shumbha declared war on the Goddess, his fate was sealed.

Shri Ramkrishna used to say, "If Mother gets angry on you, no power on the Earth or beyond can save you."

That means Shumbha was a real fighter. He never surrendered and died fighting with the Goddess.

XI. THE PRAISE OF NARAYANI

The sage said,

"After the great demon was slain, Indra and the other divine beings, led by the Fire God Agni, beamed with joy and brightening the four directions, commenced praising the Goddess Katyayani.

"Be pleased, O Goddess, who removes all the troubles of the people who have taken asylum with you. Be pleased, O Mother of the world. Be pleased, O master of the world.

Be pleased and protect this universe. You are the master of the movable and immovable world.

O Goddess, with great valiance, you are the support of this world because you are settled in the form of Mother Earth. You nurture these worlds as water.

You are Vaishnavi with unlimited valor. You are the essential seed of the universe and the fundamental nature of the universe Goddess, and you lure the entire world.

When you are pleased, you give salvation.

O Goddess, all the branches of learning, all arts, and all women are factions of you.

O Mother, you have filled the whole world. How can we say anything better than this to praise you?

O Goddess, the Vedas have described you as omnipresent, the bestower of wealth and salvation. What more can be said about you?

We salute you, O Narayani, who lives in all beings as intelligence and bestows heaven and salvation.

We salute you, O Narayani, who are the most sanctified amongst sanctified, giver of prosperity, and protector of the people who take asylum with you.

We salute you, O Narayani, who is in the form of all arts, gives measures of time and has the power of merging the worlds.

We salute you, O Narayani, who are the most sanctified amongst sanctified, giver of prosperity, and protector of the people who take asylum with you.

We salute you, O Narayani, who are the primary cause of the genesis, nurturing, and destruction of this universe and who are the most ancient supporter of the three qualities, but who are beyond these qualities.

We salute you, O Narayani, who are always ready to protect those who take asylum with you and who remove the troubles of all.

We salute you, O Narayani, in the form of Brahmani, sitting in an airship driven by swans and killing the enemy by sprinkling water from the *pooja* pot.

We salute you, O Narayani, in the form of Maheshwari, adorned with a trident, crescent, great snake, and sitting atop a big bull.

We salute you, O Narayani, in the form of innocent Kaumari, with enormous power and surrounded by peacocks.

We salute you, O Narayani, in the form of Vaishnavi, adorned with conch, *chakra*, mace, and *shaarng*.[31]

We salute you, O Narayani, in the form of the sanctified boar, who is holding the earth with its tusks, and wields a vast *chakra* in Her hand.

We salute you, O Narayani, in the form of Narsinhi (Half lion-half female), who slaughtered the demons and protected the world.

We salute you, O Narayani, in the form of Aindri, with one thousand glistening eyes, with crown and Vajra, who destroyed the army of the demons and slew Vrutrasura.

We salute you, O Narayani, as Shivduti with a terrifying form, who shrieks and has massacred the grand army of demons.

We salute you o Narayani, as Chamunda, who has a horrifying appearance because of Her teeth, who is

---

[31] Vishnu's bow.

adorned with a garland of human skulls, and who annihilated Mundasura.

We salute you O Narayani, as Lakshmi, Lajja, Mahavidya, Shraddha, Pushti, Swadha, Dhruva, Maharatri, and Mahamaya.

Bless us O Narayani, as Saraswati manifest in intelligence, the great Lakshmi, dark-natured Babhravi, bestower of luck Ishwari.

Protect us from the great terrors O Durga, who is manifest in all, the master of the world, and all powers.

O Katyayani, let your beautiful face with three eyes protect us from the five elements.

O Bhadrakali, let your fierce trident, which crushed the demons protect us from all fears for all eternity.

O Goddess with the bell that beat the demons with its sound protect us like a mother protecting her children.

We salute you, Chandika. Let your sword bathed in the blood and flesh of demons work for our welfare.

If you are pleased, you destroy all ailments, and if you are angry, you destroy all gifts.

Those who have taken asylum do not have any fear, but they can give asylum to others.

O Ambika, you are one, but you took many forms to fight the demons who are the enemies of the just. Who else can do that?

The sixty-four branches of learning, the six sciences, the theosophical books, the Vedas, the great sentences,[32] all these help us, but none can free this world from the darkness of ignorance.

Wherever there are demons and poisonous cobras, wherever there are enemies and thieves, wherever there is a great fire, or we are in the deep sea, you are there to protect and nurture this world.

You protect this universe, so you are the master (*vishvaswamini*). You bear this universe so are the soul of the universe (*vishvatmika*).

The supporters of the universe are humble before you, so you are worshiped by the universe (*vishvavandhya*).

O Goddess, be pleased with us. As you protected us by killing the demons, protect us from our enemy forever. Annihilate the disasters born from the sins of this world.

O Goddess who removes the troubles of the entire universe, O adorable to the universe, be pleased with them who have prostrated before you in devotion. Be benevolent to all."

---

[32] *Pradnyanam Brahm* (Consciousness is Brahman) from *Rigveda*, *Aham Brahmasmi* (I am Brahman) from *Yajurveda*, *Tatvamasi* (Thou art That) from Samveda and *Ayamatma Brahma* (My soul is Brahman) from *Atharvaveda*).

The Goddess said,

"O Gods, I am eager to bestow boons. Whatever you wish for the welfare of this world, do ask. I shall give it to you."

The Gods said,

"O master of the three worlds, as you annihilated our enemy and removed our troubles, do this in the future also."

The Goddess said,

"In the 28th section of Vaivasvata Manvantara,[33] more incarnations of Shumbha and Nishumbha will emerge.

Then I, born to the cowherd Nanda and Yashoda and living on the Vindhya mountain, shall annihilate them.

Again, I shall appear in a terrible form on this earth in the same era and annihilate demons named Vaiprachitta.

When I devour those demons, my teeth will be red like pomegranate seeds.

Then Gods in heavens and the mortals will praise me, addressing me as "Raktadantika" (One with Red Teeth).

Then there will be drought for one hundred years. I shall appear again after the invocation by the sages.

I shall look at the sages with a hundred eyes so people will praise me as "Shatakshi" (One with a Hundred Eyes).

---

[33] Manu's times. There are fourteen Manus.

Till it rains again, I shall nurture this world with the vegetation born from my body.

Then I shall be known as "Shakambhari."[34]

In the same era, I shall kill a demon named Durgasura, and my name "Durgadevi," will be renowned in this world.

Again, I shall appear in a terrible form to protect the sages and slay the demons.

Then the sages will prostrate themselves and praise me. I shall be famous as "Bhimadevi" then.

When a demon named Arun brings strife to the three worlds, I shall appear in the form of innumerable six-legged insects.

I shall obliterate that demon, and people will praise me as "Bhramari."[35]

Thus, whenever the demons cause trouble in this world, I shall appear and eradicate them.

Thus ends the eleventh chapter of the *Devi Mahatmya* called *The Praise of Narayani.*

---

[34]   *Shak* is vegetable.

[35]   *Bhramar* means insect, a bee to be exact.

Notes

This chapter features praise from the Gods again. The mantras are powerful. However, in my opinion, the Mother Goddess listens to prayers in every language.

The Goddess reveals to us in this chapter that She will emerge in the future, but these forms are mystical. There is a mention of Nanda's daughter. According to legends, Krishna was born in prison. Kansa was going to kill him, so his father, Vasudeva, took the child to Nanda's house.

Nanda's wife had given birth to a female child. He brought that child to the prison. When Kansa came to murder the child in the morning, the child escaped his grasp, and the Mother Goddess appeared. It was this child, born to Nanda and Yashoda, who is called Nandā. This part was either composed after the *Bhagavata* or after the Krishna cult increased in popularity.

Another mysterious form is Bhramari. She manifests in the form of thousands of bees and will be called Bhramari. Later, She will appear as vegetation to nourish the world and will be called Shakambhari.

XII. THE SENTENCE OF THE GODDESS

The Goddess said,

"Whoever praises me with these *Narayani Stotra* will have all his troubles removed by me.

Whoever recites the slaying of Madhu and Kaitabha, the felling of Mahishasura, and the killing of Shumbha and Nishumbha will also be protected.

Those who listen with devotion and concentration about my greatness on the eighth, ninth, and fourteenth day of the fortnight will be absolved of all sins.

No calamity born of sins will emerge. They will not experience poverty, and their nearest and dearest ones will never part from them.

They will not have any fear of the enemy, thief, or the king. They need not fear weapons, fire, or water.

So, all devotees should read or listen to this *stotra* which explains my greatness with total devotion and concentration.

The reading or listening of this greatness will annihilate all troubles and the three kinds of agitations.

I never leave this place and always dwell wherever people read this or listen to this systematically while offering sacrifice.

The offering of sacrifice, worship, and the fire ritual should be accompanied by the reading or listening of this *stotra* which speaks of my greatness.

I accept with affinity all sacrificial worship, performed knowingly and unknowingly, and the fire ritual accompanied by recitation or listening.

In the season of Sharad[36] one should listen to this and receive my boon. The devotee will be free from all troubles, and their coffers will be filled with money and grain. There is no doubt about that.

When one listens to these praises, my benevolent emergence, and my courage in battle, that devotee becomes free from all fears

After listening to this, all enemies are annihilated, the devotee prospers, and his or her clan keeps on growing.

If one must pacify situations, if one has nightmares or is afflicted by inauspicious stars,[37] they should listen to my greatness.

---

[36] When nine nights are celebrated in praise of the Mother Goddess.

[37] A horoscope with negative planetary afflictions.

Then all is alleviated, and nightmares become dreams of good omens.

When a child is suffering from epilepsy, when people cannot reach an agreement, this *stotra* helps.

This *stotra* calms the nerves of sinners. Just by reading it, the evil spirits like demons, ghosts, etc. are obliterated.

Thus, this *stotra* about my eminence brings one into proximity with me.

Whatever rewards are achieved by offering the best of animals, flowers, offerings, incense, lamps (along with feast to the Brahmins), fire rituals, water rituals, and other consumables offered to me for one year, are also achieved by simply reading or listening to this *stotra* which relates my greatness.

If one listens to the stories of my emergence or sings about them, their sins are removed, they become healthy, and they are protected from dangerous animals.

If one listens to how I killed the wicked demons on the battlefield, there is no fear of enemies.

Whenever you or Brahmadeva sings praises, they also will bestow excellent judgments by reading.

If one is caught in a forest fire, if thieves surround one in a deserted land, or if one is tied by enemies,

If an elephant, lion, or tiger is chasing one, if one faces the death penalty, or is being taken to jail or the gallows,

If one's boat is caught in a stormy sea, or one is facing an enemy armed with powerful weapons,

And if one is suffering from any other kinds of trouble or is in pain, they are freed from all problems if they just remember this part.

If one just recalls my saga, then lions and thieves will run away from him."

The sage said,

"The great and valiant Goddess Chandika spoke thus and disappeared while the divine beings looked at Her.

As their enemies were annihilated, the Gods started receiving their portions from the fire ritual and returned to their duties.

When the demon Shumbha, who possessed incomparable valor, was about to destroy the world, and the mighty warrior Nishumbha was dead, the remaining demons returned to the netherworld.

In this way, O King, even if the Goddess is always present, She manifests in a form to protect and nurture the world.

This world is tempted by the illusion of the Goddess, and She is the Creator.

If She is pleased, She bestows wealth, and if you pray to Her, She provides mystic knowledge for you.

O King, with Her forms as Mahakali, Mahadevi, and Mahamari She has filled the entire universe.

In the beginning, She was Aja (One Who is Never Born), and at the time of being, She nurtures all living creatures.

At the time of the deluge, She is Mahamari. In all ages, she is Sanatani.

When one is progressing, She is Lakshmi who provides prosperity, and when one is experiencing failure, the Goddess becomes Alakshmi.[38]

If one worships Her with praise, offering flowers and incense, She systematically bestows wealth, children, righteousness, and finally salvation."

Thus ends the twelfth chapter of the *Devi Mahatmya* called *The Sentence of the Goddess.*

Notes

This chapter emphasizes the importance of the entire book. Almost every Sanskrit text bestows the different kinds of fruits (rewards) that one obtains after reading, reciting, or listening to the content. It is said that unless one finishes with the *phalshruti* (the fruits of this *stotra*), then his or her ritual is not complete.

---

[38] The opposite of Lakshmi.

XIII. GRANTING BOONS TO THE KING AND THE MERCHANT

The sage said,

"In this way, O King, I have narrated the exquisite emergence of the Goddess to you.

The Goddess who bears this world is all-powerful. She, who is the illusion of lord Vishnu, provides the knowledge of salvation.

She tempted you, this merchant, and many others who had a solid sense of purpose. She will tempt many more in the future.

O King, surrender to Parameshwari. When people worship Her, She bestows wealth, heaven, and salvation."

Markandeya said,

"When he heard that Sage who had done difficult penance, King Suratha, saluted that great soul.

O great sage, the king who was sorrowful due to the loss of his kingdom, and the merchant who was sad because of his kindred immediately went to do the penance.

Seeking the immediate appearance of Amba, the king and the merchant began to do penance on the sandbank of the river by reciting the *Devi Sukta*.

They sculpted the Goddess's idol from mud and worshiped Her with flowers, incense, and other offerings like the fire ritual.

They concentrated on Her by controlling their organs, practicing total fasting, and offered Her sacrifice decorated with their blood.

After performing penance of three years with total devotion, the Mother Goddess Chandika appeared in person before them."

The Goddess said.

"Whatever you wish for O King and O high borne one (the merchant), I shall grant your wishes gladly."

Markandeya said,

"The king asked for a vast kingdom in his next life and for his enemy to be destroyed since he had lost his kingdom in this life.

The merchant had realized that there was no point in owning anything, as he had practiced renunciation, so he asked for eternal knowledge."

The Goddess said,

"O King, you will regain your kingdom shortly.

You will defeat your enemy, and there will not be any trouble for you in the future.

When your time on this earth is over, you will be born again to the Sun God.

And you will be famous in this world as Sawarni Manu.

O great merchant, I will grant you your request. You will acquire the knowledge of salvation."

Markandeya said,

"After granting them boons, the Goddess, praised by those two, disappeared.

In this way, the great Kshatriya King Suratha, after obtaining the boon from the Goddess, will be born again to the Sun God and will become the eighth Manu named Sawarni."

Thus ends the thirteenth chapter of the *Devi Mahatmya* called *Granting Boons to the King and the Merchant*.

******

This *Devi Mahatmya* is a part of Markandeya Mahapurana's *Savarnik Manvantara*.

Notes

This chapter is the last, and it speaks of the merchant and the king obtaining their desires. The king wanted his lost kingdom, but the merchant had grown weary of the world's affairs, so he asked for knowledge and was granted that.

This chapter tells us how Savarni Manu was born. He was one of the fourteen Manus who were the first men and also lawgivers.

We find the mention of Manu in the *Rigveda*. He is equated with Vaivasvat Manu in the Vedas. Vivasvan is the name of the Sun God. Vaivasvat Manu, therefore, means 'Son of the Sun God.'

Interestingly, Savarni Manu was the son of Savarna. He is called Savarni after his mother. The *Rigveda* says that he was a great king and had a very generous temperament.

It is befitting that the *Devi Mahatmya* tells his story because he is known after his mother.

THE ARMOR OF THE GODDESS

DEVI KAVACHAM

There are armors for different Gods. In Sanskrit, they are called *kavachas*. If you wear them, you are protected. There is *Ramraksha, Datta Kavach*, and *Shiva Kavach*. The various names of a God are recited to protect different parts of the body. Of all the *kavachas*, *Devi Kavacham*, or the Armor of the Goddess, is the most comprehensive.

The sage of this *kavacha* is Brahma. The meter is *anusthubh*. The presiding deity is Chamunda.

Om Markandeya said,

"Grandfather, tell me the secret which has never been told which protects human beings from all sides."

Brahmadeva said,

"O sage, listen to the armor of the Goddess, which is a well-kept secret and is beneficial to all beings.

In this armor, there are nine Durgas. The First is Shailputri (the Daughter of the Mountain, Parvati). The second is

Brahmacharini (One Who Observes Celibacy), the third is Chandraghanta, and the fourth is Kushmanda.

The fifth is Skandmata (the mother of Skanda is Parvati). The sixth is Katyayani (the daughter of the sage Katyayana). The seventh is Kalratri. The eighth is Mahagauri.

And the ninth is Siddhidatri (One Who Gives the Desired Fruits). These are known as the Nine Durgas, and the Vedas have divulged these names.

One who is imprisoned by fire, one who is surrounded by enemies on the battlefield, one who is stranded in a remote, inaccessible place and is frightened, receives sanctuary from the Mother Goddess.

And nothing happens to them in war, nor any other kind of trouble. I do not see any fear or grief coming to them.

Whoever remembers Navadurga with devotion receives fruition (rewards).

Chamunda riding on a corpse, Varahi riding on a buffalo, Aidri riding on an elephant, Vaishnavi riding on an eagle, Maheshwari on a bull, Kaumari who has a peacock as a vehicle, Lakshmi sitting on a lotus, holding a lotus, and who is the beloved of Hari, Ishvari in Her white form riding on a bull, Brahmi adorned with many ornaments and riding on a swan, all these forms of the Mother Goddess are embodiments of motherly feelings.

They possess a conch, circular weapon, mace, power, sharp grass, a plow, *tomar*,[39] cross axe, and a lasso as their weapons.

In addition to this, they also have a spear, a trident, a *vajra*,[40] *parigh*, sword, *pettish,* and *mudgar.*

They bear these weapons to slay demons, protect their devotees, as well as protecting the welfare of the Gods.

One only has to meditate upon the forms of the Goddesses and recite the armor of the Goddess to fulfill all desires.

Let Aindri protect me from the east, and the Fire Goddess protect me from the southeast.

Let the south be protected by Varahi and Khadgdharini from the southwest. Let the west be protected by Varuni and let Mrugvahini protect the northeast.

Let my north be protected by Kauberi and let Shooldharini protect the northwest. Let the upper direction be protected by Brahmani and let the lower be protected by Vaishnavi. Let all ten directions be protected by Chamunda, who rides a cadaver.

Let Jaya be before me and Vijaya be behind me. Let Ajita be on the left side and Aparajita on the right.

---

[39] A Javelin.

[40] A weapon made from bones.

Let my tuft be protected by Dhyotini and let Uma remain in my head. Let Maladhari protect my forehead, and Yashaswini protect my eyebrows.

Let my eyes be protected by Shankhini, and let Dwarvasini protect my ears. Let Kalika protect my cheeks and Shankari protect the base of the ears.

Let Sugandha remain in my nostrils, Churchika in my upper lip, Amrutkala in the lower lip, Saraswati in my tongue. Let Kaumari be in my teeth, Chandika in my throat, Chitraghanta in the bone of the throat, Mahamaya in the hollow of the head, and protect them.

Let Kamakshi protect the chin. Let Sarvamangala protect my speech, Let Bhadrakali remain in my neck, Dhanurdhari in my spinal cord.

Let Khadgdharini remain in my shoulders, Vajradharini in my biceps, Dandini in my hands, Ambika in my fingers, and protect them.

Let Shuleshwari protect my nails, Naleshwari my armpits, and let Mahadevi, who removes all grief in the mind, protect my nipples.

Let Lalitadevi remain in my heart, Shuldharini in my stomach, Kamini in my naval, Guhyeshwari in my anus, and protect them.

Let my private parts be protected by Bhutnatha, Meghvahana protect my thighs, and let Bhagvati remain to my west, Vindhyavasini to my knees, and protect them.

Let Mahabala, who grants all wishes, protect my groin. Let Narsinhi protect my ankles and let Amitdhyuti protect the back of my feet.

Let Shridhari protect my toes. Let the soles of my feet be protected by Talwasini. Let Danstrakarali protect the toenails, and let Urdhwakeshini protect my hair.

Let Kauberi protect the roots of body hair. Let Vagishwari protect my skin. Let Parvati protect my blood, bones, nerves, flesh, and fat.

Let Kalratri protect my intestines. Let Mukuteshwari protect my pancreas. Let Padmavati live in the cocoons of lotus in my body and protect them. Let Chudamani protect my Kafa.[41]

Let Jvalamukhi protect the fire of my nails. Let Abhedhya protect the joints. Let Brahmani protect my semen, and let Chhatreshvari protect my shadow.

Let Dharmadharini protect my ego, mind, and intelligence. Let Her protect my five *pranas, pran, apan, vyan, udan, and saman*.[42]

Let Yogini protect my five senses, touch, sight, smell, noise, and taste. Let Narayani protect my three qualities, *satva* (goodness), *raja* (moderate), and *tama* (dark).

---

[41] According to Ayurveda, everybody has *kafa, pitta*, and *vata* present in his or her body in a proportion. If the proportion is imbalanced the body becomes sick.

[42] According to Yoga there are five forces of the wind. The wind that comes in is *pran*, The wind that goes out is *apan*.

Let Varahi protect my life span. Let Vaishnavi protect my religion.[43] Let all mothers protect my success, fame, and wealth.

Let Indrani protect my clan. Let Chandika protect my animals.[44] Let Mahalakshmi protect my sons. Let Bhairavi protect my wife.

Let Dhaneshwari protect my wealth. Let Kaumari protect my daughters. Let Kshemakari protect my path and let Vijaya always remain with me and protect me.

Let whatever is remaining unprotected by this armor be protected by the absolver of sins, Jayanti.

O Brahmarushi,[45] because of your devotion, I have given you this all protective and wish-fulfilling armor which is a vital secret.

If one wants to save oneself, one should not take a single step without protecting one's body with this armor.

If this armor covers one, wherever he goes, he obtains wealth and wish-fulfilling victory.

Whatever wish he has, it will be fulfilled by the recitation of these armor mantras. He becomes the richest man on this planet.

---

[43] Here religion means one's duties, not the established religions.

[44] These early people relied very much on the animals they had like cows, buffaloes, and horses.

[45] Markandeya was one of the top sages so he is addressed as Brahmarushi.

This armor of the Goddess is unattainable even to the Gods. If anyone reads it three times in a day after being purified, they will achieve divinity. They will become unconquerable and will live in this world for a hundred years.

If one reads this armor, any abscess, smallpox, or ailment is cured. Any poison of either the immobile (plants), mobile (reptiles), or artificial creation (chemicals) is neutralized.

Black magic, the effects caused by insects or small creatures living in the earth or sky, and any other incidental troubles are also negated.

Innate or hereditary problems, the trouble caused by Shakini, Dakini, planets, spirits Yakshas, Gandharvas, and Rakshasas are likewise removed.

If one has the armor in his mind, Brahmarakshasa,[46] Vetal, Kushmand, and Bhairav disappear.

If the devotee reciting the armor is a king, his fame grows, and he attains success in the land, adorned with his glory.

One has to read these armor mantras first and then read the seven hundred mantras of the *Devi Mahatmya*. He automatically gets the fruits of reciting Chandi mantras without any effort.

As long as this earth remains, with its mountains, woods, and forests, his sons, grandsons, and other descendants will continue living.

---

[46] A spirit of a dead Brahmin.

After his death, he receives an eternal status by the grace of Mahamaya, which is unattainable even to the Gods."[47]

---

[47]   In some variations there is a line which says "He lives with Shiva happily."

THE TRIAD OF SECRETS

THE MAIN SECRET

PRADHANIKA RAHASYAM

The sage is *sumedha*. The meter is *anusthubha*. The presiding deity is Ādishakti Mahalakshmi. To be read after the *Devi Mahatmya*.

The King said,

"Lord, you have told me about the different incarnations of Chandika. Now tell me about Her fundamental primary nature.

O Brahmin, which aspect of the Goddess should I worship? What is the method for it? Tell it to me who is humbly asking you."

The sage said,

"O King, this is an important secret which should not be told to anyone. But you are my devotee, as well the Goddess's devotee, so I cannot keep anything from you.

The fundamental nature of this universe is the great Goddess Mahalakshmi, who has an aim and has three qualities, but Her unaimed essence has occupied the entire universe.

O King, She bears in Her Hands, a *matuling,*[48] a mace, a betel pot, and a *khet.*[49] On Her head, She bears a serpent, a *linga,* and a *yoni.*[50]

She has a luster like molten gold. She has filled this world, which was a vast void with Her shining warmth and purified ornaments of gold.

When She saw the void of the world, She adopted another form with Her dark (*tama*) quality.

She became like black soot with fangs, but She was beautiful, with Her widened eyes and narrow midriff.

She held a sword, a betel pot, a skull, and a shield in Her four hands. She had a garland of skulls around Her neck and Her head.

Mahalakshmi said to that dark-natured woman, "I shall give you names and duties accordingly.

The names are Mahamaya, Mahakali, Mahamari, Kshudha (Hunger), Trusha (Thirst), Nidra (Sleep), Ekweera, Kalratri, and Duratyaya.

---

[48] A type of flower.

[49] A wedge.

[50] Together they represent Shiva and Parvati. This is the description of Shri Mahalakshmi who resides in Kolhapur, Maharashtra.

These names are allocated to you according to the duties of the names. Anyone who recites these names, with the duties attached to the meaning, becomes happy."

"Thus saying O King, Mahalakshmi took another form with Her good (*satwa*) quality which was white, like the moon.

She held a garland of flowers, an elephant goad, *veena,*[51] and a book in Her hands. Mahalakshmi bestowed that great woman with names.

The names were Mahavidya, Mahavani, Bharati, Vaq, Saraswati, Aarya, Brahmi, Kamdhenu, Vedgarbha, and Dhishwari.

Then Mahalakshmi said to Mahakali and Mahasarasvati, "Now you create pairs the same as you."

Mahalakshmi created a splendid couple like the core of gold seated on a lotus.

Mahalakshmi called the male "Brahma, Vidhi, Virench, Dhat" and called the woman "Shri, Padma, Kamala, and Lakshmi."

Mahakali and Mahasarasvati also created their pairs. I shall tell you about their appearance and names.

Mahakali created a pale man with a blue-colored throat and reddened biceps who wore a crescent atop his head and an equally pale woman.

---

[51] A musical instrument.

That male is Rudra, Shankara, Sthanu, Kapardi, and Trilochana,[52] and the woman was Vedtrayi, Vidya, Kamdhenu, Bhasha (Language), Swara (Noise), and Akshara (Letters).

And Mahasarasvati created a pale woman and a dark man. I shall tell you their names.

The names of the male are Vishnu, Krishna, Rushikesh, Vasudeva, and Janardana. The woman was Uma, Gauri, Sati, Chandi, Sundari, Subhaga, and Shivā.

In this way, the three Goddesses (Mahalakshmi, Mahasarasvati, and Mahakali) obtained their male forms. Only wise people know this. The others, who create discrimination, do not know this secret.[53]

O King, Mahalakshmi gave Vedatrayi as wife to Brahmadeva, Varadagauri as wife to Rudra, and Shri as wife to Vasudeva.

Brhmadeva created the egg containing the universe with the help of Sarasvati, and the valiant Rudra broke it with the assistance of Gauri.

Then, O King, In the egg containing the universe, different functions, the movable and the immovable, and the five elements appeared.

Vishnu nurtured the universe with the help of Lakshmi. In this way, Mahalakshmi, who has no beginning, has

---

[52] All Shiva's names.

[53] The names are different, but the God is one. This is an reconciliation attempt between the Vaishnavaites and the Shaivites.

mastered all Gods and Goddesses. She is inherently formless, but according to Her function, She adopts a form and bears various names. Many different names can describe Her, but the formless Goddess cannot be described by any name.

THE SECRET OF TRANSFORMATION

VAIKRUTHIKA RAHASYAM[54]

The sage said,

"I told you the main secret of the three qualities of the Goddess, namely Triguna,[55] Rajasi,[56] Tamasi,[57] and Satviki.[58] She is also called Sharva, Chandika, Durga, Bhadra, and Bhagvati.

Brahmadeva, seated on a lotus, prayed to the Goddess who had taken the form of sleep to kill Madhu and Kaitabha. She is called dark-natured Mahakali.

She has ten heads, ten hands, and ten legs. She appears terrible because of Her shining teeth and fangs, but even

---

[54] *Vikruti* means to 'modify form.' Therefore, the *Vaikrutika Rahasya* narrates the secret of the Goddess' multiple forms. But this *stotra* describes the different forms of the Goddess. In this context, it tells the reader that She is the same Goddess in different forms.

[55] Of the three qualities.

[56] Mahalakshmi.

[57] Dark natured, Mahakali.

[58] Good natured, Mahasarasvati.

then, O King, She is the presiding deity of beauty, welfare, luster, and wealth.

Wielding sword, arrow, mace, lasso, *chakra,* conch, and *bhushudi*. She holds a *parigh*,[59] a bow, and a severed head in Her hands.

She is the illusion of Vishnu, and even though it is challenging, once She is pleased, She gives all the universe to Her devotee.

One who emerged from the bodies of the Gods, She is the shining Mahalakshmi of the three qualities who killed Mahishasura.

She is fair. Her hands are blue. Her breasts are white. Her midriff, legs, and thighs are red. She is in an intoxicated state. Her middle part is of many colors like this earth. She wears colorful garlands, ornaments, and dresses. She enjoys many kinds of scents and fragrances. She possesses beauty, good luck, and luster.

Anyone who worships Mahalakshmi, representing all Gods, will become the master of all the people and Gods.

She has thousands of hands, but only eighteen are visible, and She is very charming. She holds the following weapons in Her hands; a garland, a lotus, an arrow, a sword, a *vajra*, a mace, a *chakra*, a trident, a *parashu*, a conch, a bell, and a lasso.

---

[59] *Parigh* literally means circumference.

She also has a staff, a shield, a bow, a betel pot, and a *puja* pot in her hands. She is seated on a lotus.

The one who emerged from the body of Gauri, has only goodness as Her quality. This is the killer of Shumbha, known as Mahasarasvati.

O King, She is the bearer of *shula* and in Her eight hands She holds a *chakra*, an arrow, sharp grass, a conch, a bell, a plough, and a bow.

Anyone who worships this Goddess, the killer of Shumbha and Nishumbha, is given all knowledge by Her.

O King, I have told you all about the different forms of the Mother. Now I shall tell you how to worship the Mother and Her different forms.

When you worship Mahalakshmi, worship Mahakali at the south, and Mahasaraswati to the north, and the three couples behind.

Place Brahmadeva with Sarasvati in the center, place Shiva and Parvati on the right side, and place Vishnu and Lakshmi on the left. And keep three idols in the front.

In the center, the Goddess with eighteen hands. To the left, the Goddess with ten hands, to the right Lakshmi with eight hands. The three are to be systematically worshiped.

When worshiping the Goddess with eighteen hands, worship the Goddess with ten hands to the south, and the Goddess with the eight hands to the north.

When worshiping the Goddess with ten hands, worship the God of time in the south and the God of death in the north to remove all obstacles.

When worshiping the killer of Shumbha, the Goddess with eight hands, Nava Durga[60] and Rudra Vinayaka should be worshiped.

Mahalakshmi should be worshiped with the mantra "*namo Daivyei.*" When one is worshiping Mahakali or Mahasaraswati the mantras uttered to invoke them (in the *Devi Mahatmya*) should be recited.

You should worship the Goddess with eighteen hands who killed Mahishasura because Mahalakshmi is called Mahasarasvati and Mahakali.

Anyone who worships Mahishasurmardini, who is the presiding deity of good deeds and sins and the Goddess of all the worlds, becomes the master of this universe .

Chandika, who bears all the worlds and who is very kind towards Her devotees, should be worshiped with offerings of water, flowers, fragrant pastes, and ornaments.

There should be incense, oil lamp, and food offerings. Kshatriyas[61] like you can offer meat with blood and wines also.

One should bow again and again, should take water, sandalwood paste, and betel with camphor.

---

[60] The Nine Forms of Durga.

[61] Warrior caste.

One who has become one with the Goddess, the demon Mahishasura with the severed head, should be worshiped at the front of the Goddess, to the left.

The lion of the Goddess, who is in all movable and immovable beings, who represents the duties and is very powerful, should be worshiped to the right side.

Then one should fold his hands and invoke the Goddess with all three episodes or only the middle episode (*Madhyam Charitra*). It should not be either only first (*Pratham Charitra*) or only the best episode (*Uttam Charitra*).

No biography should be left incomplete. Leaving it incomplete will produce obstacles for the devotee. Alternatively, one can recite the *stotras* and praise the Mother of the Worlds.

One should circumambulate, prostrate and fold his hands, and with a conscious mind, ask for forgiveness from the Goddess again and again.

Offer sesame with *ghee* to the fire after reciting the mantras or do the fire ritual with Chandi Mantras and honor Chandika for wellbeing.

With a peaceful mind and folded hands, bow before Chandika to establish Her in your heart and meditate on Her for a long time to become one with Her.

Anyone who worships the Goddess like this daily, lives well and after death unites with the Goddess.

Anyone who does not worship this Chandika, who is very kind towards Her devotees, has all the benefits of his good deeds burnt by Parameshvari.

So, O King, systematically worship Chandika, who is the Master of all the worlds, and you obtain all the pleasures of this world.

THE SECRET OF THE IDOLS

MOORTI RAHASYAM

(The sage is *sumedha*. The meter is *anusthubha*. The presiding deity is Mahalakshmi in the form of Nandā. This *stotra* is to be recited after the *Devi Mahatmya*.)

The sage said,

"Anyone who worships Nandā who would be born to Nanda, the cowherd king, should praise Her with *stotras* and meditate on Her. Then everything in the three worlds will be given to him.

She shines like gold and wears lustrous golden clothes adorned with a gilded belt and golden ornaments.

She holds a lotus, an elephant goad, a lasso in Her four hands, and is seated on a golden lotus. She is called Indira, Kamala, Lakshmi, and Shri.

I have told you about Raktadantika. I shall tell you about Her nature which removes all fears.

She wears red clothes, and her complexion is red. She is decorated with red ornaments and bears red weapons. She has red eyes and red hair, which makes Her terrifying to behold.

She has sharp red nails, red fangs, and red hands, but she bestows affection on her devotees like a devoted wife.

She is broad like this earth, and her breasts are large. Like the mountains of Meru, and are very plump and attractive.

With her firm, beautiful, and lovely breasts, She satisfies the thirst of her devotees.

This Goddess carries a sword, a betel pot, sharp grass, and a plow in Her hands. She is also famous as Raktachamunda and Yogeshwari.

She has occupied the entire universe, so one who worships Her also occupies the movable and immovable universe.

Anybody who praises the body of the Goddess Raktadantika is rewarded by the Goddess like a wife rewards her beloved husband.

Shakambhari has blue skin, eyes like a blue lotus, a deep naval, and a flat tummy with three folds.

She has firm, round, and plump breasts. She has arrows in Her lower right fist and a lotus in her upper hand. She sits on a lotus.

She holds vegetables in Her hands with leaves, flowers, fruits, and roots full of juice which remove all hunger, thirst, old age, and death.

Parameshwari bears a lustrous bow. Shakambhari is also famous as Shatakshi and Durga.

If one praises, worships, recites the names, or meditates on Shakambhari, he or she immediately receives an infinite supply of food and drinks.

The one with blue luster, shining fangs, wide eyes, and oval-shaped plump breasts is Bhimadevi.

She holds a sword, a drum, a human skull, and a wine pot in Her hands. She is the one who fulfills all desires and is also known as Ekveera and Kalratri.

Because of the aura around Her, it is difficult to see the Goddess, for She also has a multi-colored luster and holds multi-colored bees in Her hands. She is praised as Bhramari and Mahamari.

O King, if you praise Chandika's idols, as I have told you, they become Kamdhenu.[62]

This narration concerning the divine idols is highly confidential, and you should never tell anyone about it. But you can read it or recite it with your full attention.

I have told you how to meditate on the Goddess, which is a secret even among other secrets and is all wish-fulfilling. Preserve this in your heart.

---

[62] The divine cow which fulfills all desires.

A PRAYER FOR FORGIVENESS.

After reciting the *Devi Mahatmya*, one must recite this prayer again and again. There may be mistakes in the recital, which could anger the Goddess. Therefore, with total concentration, one has to read or recite this prayer. After all, She is the Mother, so She will definitely forgive Her devotee.

I commit thousands of mistakes every day. O Parameshvari, forgive me assuming that I am but one servant of thine.

I do not know how to invoke you. I do not know how to conclude. Forgive me, Parameshvari. I do not know how to worship also.

O Goddess, I have performed the worship without proper mantras, without rituals, and without devotion, but let it be perfect in my case.

There is no sinner like me, and there is no absolver of sins like you. Knowing this, O Mahadevi, do whatever you want to.

Even after committing hundreds of mistakes, if one says "Jagadamb" (O Mother of the World), he reaches a state which is unattainable even to Gods like Brahmadeva.

O Mother, I am a defaulter, but I have surrendered to you. Please be kind to me. Mother, do as you will.

Whatever wrongs I have committed due to ignorance, forgetfulness, or by accident, please forgive me, Mother, and be pleased.

Kameshwari, Mother of the World, embodiment of goodness, inner mind, and ego, accept this *puja* kindly and be pleased.

While reciting I may have missed a syllable, word, or another inflection. Forgive me, O Goddess, for that.

Any lapse, such as punctuation or notes, may have been wrong. Forgive me, O Goddess, for that.

SIDDHA KUNJIKA STOTRAM

This is a powerful *stotram* to invoke the Mother. This is woven around the *mantra* "*Oum aim hreem kleem chamundayai vichche.*"

Shiva said,

"O Goddess, please listen to the excellent *kunjika stotram*. Because of its mantric power, it immediately rewards one with the fruits of worshiping the Mother.

You need not read the *kawacha*, *argala stotram, keelakam,* or any of the secrets. No *suktas*, *nyas*,[63] nor any other rituals are required. If you recite the *kunjika stotram*, you receive all the fruits of Durga Worship.

This is a vital secret. It is unattainable even to the Gods. Parvati Herself generated this *Stotram*.

---

[63] This is supposed to be done before *Devi Mahatmya*. It is like a foundation.

This *stotram,* when recited, can kill, and like magic, it can make a person yours, cause anything to stagnate, and remove anything instantly.

I salute the Mother in the terrible form who killed the demon Madhu, the killer of Kaitabha. Salutations to the Goddess who killed Mahishasura.

I salute the Mother who killed Shumbha, the annihilator of Nishumbha. Awaken Mother and bring fruition to my prayers.

As (*eim*) you are the universe, and as (*hreem*) you look after the world. As (*kleem*), you are the embodiment of desire. I salute you as the source of everything.

As the killer of Chanda, you are Chamunda (*yai*), which denotes you as a bestower of boons (*vichche*) meaning you are a protector. I salute you in the form of mantra.

Dhaam dheem dhoom as one with dreadlocks and wife. *Vaam veem voom* as the supreme Goddess of the spoken word. *Kraam kreem kroom* as the Goddess Kalika. *Shaam sheem shoom* bring good to me.

Hoom hoom hoomkar as the sound *hoom. Jam jam jam*, as the sound made in pride. *Bhraam bhreem bhroom* as the good Bhairavi. I salute you Mother Bhavani.

Am, kam cham, tam, tam, pam, yam, sham, veem doom, aim veem, ham, ksham gather at the edge of the sound *dhee*; gather, enkindle, and consume this!

Paam peem poom as the perfect Parvati. *Khaam kheem khoom*) as Khechari.[64] *Saam seem soom* as the Goddess in *Saptashati*. I implore you to bring about the effects of these mantras.

This *stotram* is used to awaken the mantras. O Mother Parvati, maintain its secrecy and do not give it to non-devotees.

If one reads the seven hundred couplets without reciting *kunjika stotram*, it is of no use."

---

[64] The Mother as a mule.

ABOUT THE AUTHOR

 Raghupati Bhatt has been a professor of English and a freelancer since 1975. He has written on various themes for newspapers and republished them as books. To date, Raghupati has published eleven books. This is his latest book.

Raghupati, now retired, was an associate professor for GVM's College of Commerce in Ponda Goa. His publications written for Numen Books, *India's Glory* and *Bhagvad Gita* were exclusive.

Raghupati lives in Ponda Goa with his wife Vijaya.